FAST TRACK

EXAM PREP NOTES

AWS Certified Cloud Practitioner

[CLF-C01]

ACKNOWLEDGMENTS

Welcome to the Fast Track Exam Notes for AWS Certified Cloud Practitioner (CLF-C01) from CLOUDAI Academy.

The primary focus of creating this book is to consolidate the end-to-end precise CPP examination study materials from the official AWS website and whitepapers. The goal is to help the professionals, students and AWS/Cloud enthusiasts to prepare themselves for the CLF-C01 examination without spending their most precious time for researching on multiple unorganized and scattered study materials.

This book will encourage you to manage a very short time from your extremely busy schedule to be prepared for CCP examination, which is going to be a basic need for any IT students and professionals in the coming days.

Congratulations in advance for Successfully PASSING AWS Certified Cloud Practitioner examination.

Thanks & Regards,

CLOUDAI Academy

CONTACT US

Your opinion and feedback is extremely important for us and this is the most important knowledge source for CLOUDAI Academy to continuously improve the course and provide the best experience to our students. So feel free to mail us on clouaiacademy@gmail.com

Also the goal of CLOUDAI Academy is not only to develop courses but building a community, where all of our students can exchange their experience and knowledge along with can share and refer for new job opportunities. Please join us on Facebook by clicking https://www.facebook.com/AWS-Professionals-community-104203417993082

This will also give you a wonderful opportunity to get continuous updates on AWS world and you will be encouraged by learning others' success story.

BEST WAY TO READ THIS BOOK

Although this book is for exam notes to fast track your preparation, the course content has been designed and categorized by maintaining a proper sequence considering different domains and topics under every domain.

Before going into the technical content, it is extremely important to understand the examination pattern. So please complete chapter 1 before starting with any other chapter where the entire examination blueprint has been explained precisely.

So, it is recommended not to skip the sequence in any chapter. It is fine to read and pick any of the chapters, but better to maintain the sequence to boost your confidence level.

BONUS OFFER!!!

Bingo...Here is your bonus.

Up to **50% Discount** in *Exam simulator with 6 practice test sets with 390 questions*

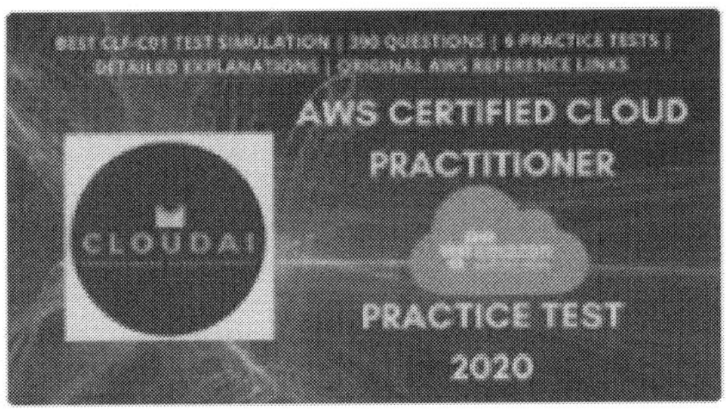

DIRECT DISCOUNTED LINK

https://www.udemy.com/course/aws-certified-cloud-practitioner-best-6-practice-exam-2020/?couponCode=CLOUDAIAWSTESTSIM

OR

COUPON CODE

CLOUDAIAWSTESTSIM

CONTENTS

OTHER COURSES

Evaluate yourself *before the final examinations is always a smart idea*

Here are the best options for you:

Study book of 7 practice test sets with 450+ question in ***Ultra low price***

https://www.amazon.com/gp/product/B08D9N43Y6?tag=books2read02-20

Exam simulator with 6 practice test sets with 390 questions [Use **up to 50%** ***DISCOUNTED link*** *or* ***COUPON CODE****]*

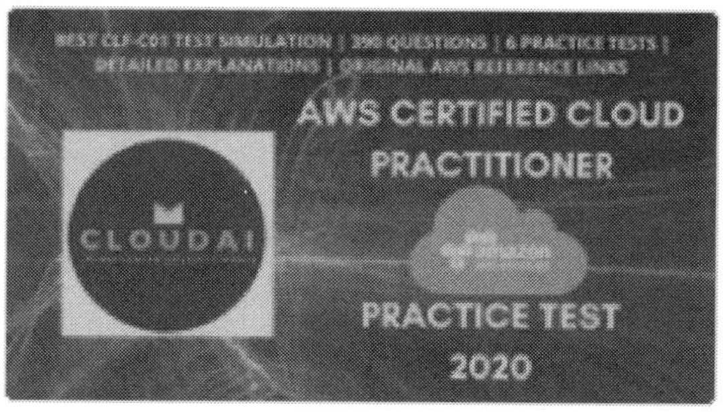

https://www.udemy.com/course/aws-certified-cloud-practitioner-best-6-practice-exam-2020/?couponCode=CLOUDAIAWSTESTSIM

OR

COUPON CODE - CLOUDAIAWSTESTSIM

CHAPTER 01 : AWS Certified Cloud Practitioner (CCP) Examination blueprint

Examination Blueprint of AWS CCP (CLF-C01)

- Who can take the examination
- Examination structure
- Knowledge areas and weightages
- Question patterns

Who can take the examination

Amazon recommends to have at least six months of work experience with AWS cloud in any role including technical, managerial, sales, purchasing, or financial.

Also Candidates should have a basic understanding of IT services and their uses in the AWS Cloud platform.

So if you are already working in AWS and planning to appear for AWS CCP you are on the right track.

Even if you are a self learner and planning to upgrade your cloud computing skill, Amazon provides a 1 year FREE AWS subscription which is enough to get a basic knowledge on different AWS services which is essential for this beginner level certification examination. Use the following link to get your 1 year FREE AWS subscription:
Free Tier AWS account sign-on link

Last but not the least, since you have purchased this course, you are already stepping into the AWS enthusiast community and the primary condition to PASS any certification exam is enthusiasm, dedication and well planned preparation.

You have the enthusiasm and you are already into a well planned exam preparation course. So you are only responsible for your dedication and we believe you have it and this course will help you to build your Success Story.

Examination structure

Here is the summary of AWS Certified Cloud Practitioner (CLF-C01) examination structure:

Time / Duration	90 Minutes
Number of Questions	65
Cost	100 USD

Negative Marking	No
Unanswered Question	Considered as Incorrect
Passing number	70% (scale : 700 of 1000)
Format	Multiple choice Multiple answer
Delivery Method	Testing center or online proctored exam
Examination booking link	CLICK HERE

Knowledge areas and weightages

This section includes domain, weightings and distribution:

DOMAIN	%
Domain 1: Cloud Concepts **1.1** Define the AWS Cloud and its value proposition **1.2** Identify aspects of AWS Cloud economics **1.3** List the different cloud architecture design principles	26%

Domain 2: Security and Compliance **2.1** Define the AWS shared responsibility model **2.2** Define AWS Cloud security and compliance concepts **2.3** Identify AWS access management capabilities **2.4** Identify resources for security support	25%
Domain 3: Technology **3.1** Define methods of deploying and operating in the AWS Cloud **3.2** Define the AWS global infrastructure **3.3** Identify the core AWS services **3.4** Identify resources for technology support	33%
Domain 4: Billing and Pricing **4.1** Compare and contrast the various pricing models for AWS **4.2** Recognize the various account structures in relation to AWS billing and pricing **4.3** Identify resources available for billing support	16%

TOTAL =	**100%**

Question patterns

There are two types of questions on the examination:

- **Multiple choice:** Has one correct response and three incorrect responses (distractors).

  Example:

  Which of the following is AWS compute service?

  - ☐ *Amazon S3*
  - ☑ *Amazon EC2*
  - ☐ *AWS VPN*
  - ☐ *AWS CloudFront*

  Answer - *Amazon EC2 (Option #2) is the correct option, since this is a compute service*

- **Multiple response:** Has two or more correct responses out of five or more options.

  Example:

  Which of the following services is part of AWS database services? (choose 2)

  - ☑ *Amazon RDS*
  - ☐ *AWS Snowball*
  - ☑ *Amazon DynamoDB*
  - ☐ *AWS Lambda*

☐ *Amazon CloudFront*

Answer - *Amazon RDS (Option #1) and Amazon DynamoDB (Option #3) are the correct answers. RDS is Relational database service and DynamoDB is a NoSQL database.*

Select one or more responses that best complete the statement or answer the question. Distractors, or incorrect answers, are response options that an examinee with incomplete knowledge or skill would likely choose. However, they are generally plausible responses that fit in the content area defined by the test objective.

NOTE:

- Unanswered questions are scored as incorrect
- There is no penalty for guessing

CLOUDAI Coffee Break

Now you must have a very clear idea about the examination blueprint and It's the most important part of PASSING any examination

CHAPTER 02 : Basics of Cloud Computing

What is Cloud Computing?

Cloud computing is the on-demand delivery of IT infrastructure resources over the Internet with pay-as-you-go pricing.

Instead of large upfront investment and spending significant time in buying, owning, and maintaining physical data centers and servers, users can access technology services, such as computing power, storage, databases and so many other services from a cloud provider like Amazon Web Services (AWS), Microsoft Azure, Google Cloud Platform (GCP)

This is nothing but one service provider company is maintaining a large infrastructure in their data center(s) and multiple users / companies are using that common infrastructure without taking responsibility and spending money on managing data centers(s) and other IT infrastructure

Cloud Computing Models

There are 3 types of cloud computing model:

1. Infrastructure as a Service (IaaS)
2. Platform as a Service (PaaS)
3. Software as a Service (SaaS)

1. **Infrastructure as a Service (IaaS)** - It contains the basic building blocks for cloud IT and typically provides access to networking features, computers (virtual or on dedicated hardware), and data storage space.

   Infrastructure as a Service provides you with the highest level of flexibility and management control over your IT resources and is most similar to existing IT resources that many IT departments and developers are familiar with today

   EXAMPLE - AWS, Azure, GCP etc.

2. **Platform as a Service (PaaS)** - It removes the need for organizations to manage the underlying infrastructure (usually hardware and operating systems) and allows you to focus on the deployment and management of your applications.

   This helps you be more efficient as you don't need to worry about resource procurement, capacity planning, software maintenance, patching or any of the other undifferentiated heavy lifting involved in running your application

EXAMPLE - AWS Elastic Beanstalk, Google App Engine

3. **Software as a Service (SaaS)** - It provides you with a completed product that is run and managed by the service provider. In most cases, people referring to Software as a Service are referring to end-user applications.

   With a SaaS offering you do not have to think about how the service is maintained or how the underlying infrastructure is managed; you only need to think about how you will use that particular piece of software.

   EXAMPLE - Microsoft Office365 , Gmail etc. are some perfect example of SaaS

>> Compare On-Premise and Cloud Computing models

On-Premise	IaaS	PaaS	SaaS
Applications	Applications	Applications	Applications
Data	Data	Data	Data
Runtime	Runtime	Runtime	Runtime
Middleware	Middleware	Middleware	Middleware

Operating System	Operating System	Operating System	Operating System
Servers	Servers	Servers	Servers
Storage	Storage	Storage	Storage
Networking	Networking	Networking	Networking
Data Center	Data Center	Data Center	Data Center

User Responsibility

Cloud Deployment Models

There are 3 types of cloud computing model:

1. Public Cloud
2. Hybrid Cloud
3. Private Cloud

1. **Public Cloud** - A cloud-based application is fully deployed in the cloud and all parts of the application run in the cloud. Applications in the cloud have either been created in the cloud or have been migrated from an existing infrastructure to take advantage of the benefits of cloud computing.

Cloud-based applications can be built on low-level infrastructure pieces or can use higher level services that provide abstraction from the management, architecting, and scaling requirements of core infrastructure.

EXAMPLE - AWS, AZURE, GCP

2. **Hybrid Cloud** - A hybrid deployment is a way to connect infrastructure and applications between cloud-based resources and existing resources that are not located in the cloud.

   The most common method of hybrid deployment is between the cloud and existing on-premises infrastructure to extend, and grow, an organization's infrastructure into the cloud while connecting cloud resources to internal systems.

   EXAMPLE - Data Center owned by the user along with archival storage in AWS

3. **Private Cloud** - Deploying resources on-premises, using virtualization and resource management tools, is sometimes called "private cloud".

   On-premises deployment does not provide many of the benefits of cloud computing but is sometimes sought for its ability to provide dedicated resources.

In most cases this deployment model is the same as legacy IT infrastructure while using application management and virtualization technologies to try and increase resource utilization.

EXAMPLE - Data Center owned by the user, VMware

Six Advantages of Cloud Computing

There are Six benefits of using Cloud Computing-

1. Trade capital expense for variable expense
2. Benefit from massive economies of scale
3. Stop guessing capacity
4. Increase speed and agility
5. Stop spending money running and maintaining data centers
6. Go global in minutes

1. **Trade capital expense for variable expense -** Instead of investing heavily in data centers and servers before you know how you're going to use them, you can pay only when you consume computing resources and pay only for how much you consume.

2. **Benefit from massive economies of scale –** By using cloud computing, you can achieve a lower

variable cost than you can get on your own. Because usage from hundreds of thousands of customers is aggregated in the cloud, providers such as AWS can achieve higher economies of scale, which translates into lower pay as-you-go prices.

3. **Stop guessing capacity** – Eliminate guessing on your infrastructure capacity needs. When you make a capacity decision prior to deploying an application, you often end up either sitting on expensive idle resources or dealing with limited capacity. With cloud computing, these problems go away. You can access as much or as little capacity as you need, and scale up and down as required with only a few minutes' notice.

4. **Increase speed and agility** – In a cloud computing environment, new IT resources are only a click away, which means that you reduce the time to make those resources available to your developers from weeks to just minutes. This results in a dramatic increase in agility for the organization, since the cost and time it takes to experiment and develop is significantly lower.

5. **Stop spending money running and maintaining data centers** – Focus on projects that differentiate your business, not the infrastructure. Cloud computing lets you focus on

your own customers, rather than on the heavy lifting of racking, stacking, and powering servers.

6. **Go global in minutes** – Easily deploy your application in multiple regions around the world with just a few clicks. This means you can provide lower latency and a better experience for your customers at minimal cost.

CLOUDAI Coffee Break

Brilliant starting

☺

Do you have a target date to finish your final preparation?
Make sure you have it

CHAPTER 03 : AWS Global Infrastructure

What is AWS Global Infrastructure?

The AWS Global Cloud Infrastructure is the most secure, extensive, and reliable cloud platform, offering over ***175 fully featured services*** from data centers globally using ***76 Availability Zones (AZ)*** in ***24 Regions.***

Every Region is a distinct geographical location and every Region has multiple AZs.

Every Availability Zone (AZ) has one or more discrete data centers with redundant power, networking, and connectivity.

Each Availability Zone (AZ) within the same Region is interconnected with high-bandwidth, low-latency networking.

https://aws.amazon.com/about-aws/global-infrastructure/

What is Regions?

- Region is a geographically distinct physical location around the world where AWS clusters data centers.
- Every Region has at least ***2 AZs*** and AWS is very close to providing at least 3 AZs in every Region.
- Each AWS Region consists of multiple, isolated, and physically separate AZ's within a geographic area.
- All of the regions does not provide all the services and there are 2 gov regions (AWS us-gov-east-1 and us-gov-west-1), which are dedicated US Government use and no other user can use these 2 regions
- Each Amazon EC2 Region is designed to be isolated from the other Amazon EC2 Regions. This achieves the greatest possible ***fault tolerance*** and ***stability***.
- When you launch an instance, you must select an AMI that's in the same Region. If the AMI is in another Region, you can copy the AMI to the Region you're using.
- You can replicate objects between different AWS Regions or within the same AWS Region:
  - ☐ **Cross-Region replication (CRR)** is used to copy objects across Amazon S3 buckets in different AWS Regions.

  - ☐ **Same-Region replication (SRR)** is used to copy objects across Amazon S3 buckets in the same AWS Region.

- Most Amazon Web Services offer a ***Regional endpoint*** that you can use to make your requests. This is nothing but a URL of the entry point for an AWS web service

  The AWS SDKs and the AWS Command Line Interface (AWS CLI) automatically use the default endpoint for each service in an AWS Region. But you can specify an alternate endpoint for your API requests.
- Computing cost varies in different Regions.
- Selecting multiple Regions increases cost.

What is the Availability Zone (AZ)?

- An Availability Zone (AZ) is one or more discrete data centers with redundant power, networking, and connectivity in an AWS Region.
- AZ's are physically separated by a meaningful distance, many kilometers, from any other AZ.
- All AZ's in an AWS Region are interconnected with high-bandwidth, low-latency networking
- All traffic between AZ's is encrypted
- The network performance is sufficient to accomplish synchronous replication between AZ's
- If an application is partitioned across AZ's, companies are better isolated and protected from issues such as power outages, lightning strikes, tornadoes, earthquakes and more.

- AZ's give customers the ability to operate production applications and databases that are more highly available, fault tolerant, and scalable than would be possible from a single data center.
- Using a Load Balancer request can be sent only to the healthy AZs and can be bypassed any unhealthy AZs, which make your architecture ***fault tolerant***.
- Elastic IP also makes AWS ***fault tolerant*** by mapping the IP address to a healthy AZ, if current AZ becomes unhealthy.
- Selecting Multiple AZs increases the AWS infrastructure cost.
- Resources are distributed across the Availability Zones for a Region.

What is the Edge Location?

- Edge location is a data center owned by AWS trusted partners that have direct connection with AWS network.
- There are 205 Edge Locations available globally
- Reduce network latency of Content Delivery Network by caching content and allow users to access content from nearby Edge Location.
- ***Regional Edge Locations*** stores relatively less frequently accessed data once removed from Edge locations.

- Regional Edge Location have higher cache size than Edge Location
- There are 11 Edge Locations available globally
- AWS Content Delivery Network (CDN) connect to Edge Locations through Regional Edge Locations

CLOUDAI Coffee Break

"We cannot be in survival mode. We have to be in growth mode."
- Jeff Bezos

CHAPTER 04 : AWS Compute Services

What are the different AWS Compute Services?

- Amazon EC2
- AWS Lambda
- AWS Elastic Beanstalk
- Amazon Lightsail
- AWS Outposts
- EC2 Image Builder

Amazon EC2

- Amazon Elastic Compute Cloud (Amazon EC2) is a web service that provides secure, resizable compute capacity in the cloud.
- It provides you with complete control of your computing resources and lets you run on Amazon's proven computing environment.
- Amazon EC2's simple web service interface allows you to obtain and configure capacity with minimal friction.
- It is designed to make web-scale cloud computing easier for developers.

- It provides you with complete control of your computing resources and lets you run on Amazon's proven computing environment.
- Secure and resizable compute capacity in the cloud.
- Launch applications when needed without upfront commitments.
- Using Amazon EC2 eliminates your need to invest in hardware up front, so you can develop and deploy applications faster.
- Amazon EC2 enables you to scale up or down to handle changes in requirements or spikes in popularity, reducing your need to forecast traffic
- EC2 stores data in Elastic Block Storage (EBS) and Instance Storage
- Unused EC2 instance can be stopped to save cost
- Terminating EC2 instance wipe out existing customer data
- Before terminating EC2 instance it's recommended to take EBS snapshot (backup) in order to retain data
- AWS SSM (System Manager) is the default Amazon EC2 role
- AMI helps AWS customers to deploy EC2 instance with almost no time
- Using Auto-scaling EC2 instance can be added or removed automatically
- Load Balancer distribute the traffic to multiple EC2 instance

>> Amazon Machine Image (AMI)

- An Amazon Machine Image (AMI) provides the information required to launch an instance.
- You can launch multiple instances from a single AMI when you need multiple instances with the same configuration.
- You can use different AMIs to launch instances when you need instances with different configurations.
- You must specify an AMI when you launch an instance.
- You can also launch instances from an AMI if the AMI owner grants you launch permissions.
- You can copy an AMI within the same Region or to different Regions.
- When you no longer require an AMI, you can deregister it.
- After you create an AMI, you can keep it private so that only you can use it, or you can share it with a specified list of AWS accounts.
- You can purchase AMIs from a third party, including AMIs that come with service contracts from organizations such as Red Hat.
- To help categorize and manage your AMIs, you can assign custom tags to them.

- There is no additional cost to create or manage an AMI
- AMI reduce time and effort to create a customize compute service and the fastest way to deploy a new EC2 instance
- There 2 types of AMI:
  - ☐ **Amazon EBS-backed AMI** - To create an Amazon EBS-backed Linux AMI, start from an instance that you've launched from an existing Amazon EBS-backed Linux AMI
  - ☐ **Instance store-backed AMI** - To create an instance store-backed Linux AMI, start from an instance that you've launched from an existing instance store-backed Linux AMI

>> AWS Auto-Scaling

- AWS Auto Scaling monitors your applications and automatically adjusts capacity to maintain steady, predictable performance at the lowest possible cost.
- Using AWS Auto Scaling, it's easy to setup application scaling for multiple resources across multiple services in minutes.
- AWS Auto-Scaling supports Amazon EC2 instances and Spot Fleets, Amazon ECS tasks, Amazon DynamoDB tables and indexes, and Amazon Aurora Replicas.

- It's easy to get started with AWS Auto Scaling using the AWS Management Console, Command Line Interface (CLI), or SDK.
- AWS Auto Scaling is available at no additional charge.
- This is the key service which provides Scalability along with making your application Fault-Tolerant by adjusting the capacity.
- AWS Auto Scaling makes scaling simple with recommendations that allow you to optimize performance, costs, or balance between them.
- If you're already using Amazon EC2 Auto Scaling to dynamically scale your Amazon EC2 instances, you can now combine it with AWS Auto Scaling
- **Amazon EC2 Auto Scaling** helps you ensure that you have the correct number of Amazon EC2 instances available to handle the load for your application.
    - ☐ **Auto-scaling Group** - Collections of EC2 instances. You can specify the minimum and maximum number of instances in each Auto Scaling group.

      Depending on that auto-scaling will launch or terminate instances automatically within the defined limit
    - ☐ **Configuration templates** - You can specify information such as the AMI ID, instance type, key pair, security groups, and block device mapping for your instances.

You can specify information such as the AMI ID, instance type, key pair, security groups, and block device mapping for your instances.

- ☐ **Scaling options** - Amazon EC2 Auto Scaling provides several ways for you to scale your Auto Scaling group :
  - Maintain current instance levels at all times
  - Scale manually
  - Scale based on a schedule
  - Scale based on demand
  - Use predictive scaling

>> Elastic Load Balancer (ELB)

- Elastic Load Balancing automatically distributes incoming application traffic across multiple targets, such as Amazon EC2 instances, containers, IP addresses, and Lambda functions.
- It can handle the varying load of your application traffic in a single Availability Zone or across multiple Availability Zones.
- Provides high availability, automatic scaling, and robust security necessary to make your applications fault tolerant.

- You can privately access Elastic Load Balancing APIs from your Amazon Virtual Private Cloud (VPC) by creating VPC endpoints.
- Elastic Load Balancing guarantees a monthly availability of at least **99.99%**
- There are 3 types of Load Balancers:
  - ☐ **Application Load Balancer** - Application Load Balancer is best suited for load balancing of HTTP and HTTPS traffic and provides advanced request routing targeted at the delivery of modern application architectures, including microservices and containers.

    Operating at the individual request level ***(Layer 7)***

    Application Load Balancer routes traffic to targets within Amazon Virtual Private Cloud (Amazon VPC) based on the content of the request.
  - ☐ **Network Load Balancer** - Network Load Balancer is best suited for load balancing of Transmission Control Protocol (TCP), User Datagram Protocol (UDP) and Transport Layer Security (TLS) traffic where extreme performance is required.

    Operating at the connection level ***(Layer 4)***

Network Load Balancer routes traffic to targets within Amazon Virtual Private Cloud (Amazon VPC)

Capable of handling millions of requests per second while maintaining ultra-low latencies.

Capable of handling millions of requests per second while maintaining ultra-low latencies.

- ☐ **Classic Load Balancer** - Classic Load Balancer provides basic load balancing across multiple Amazon EC2 instances and operates at both the request level and connection level.

  Classic Load Balancer is intended for applications that were built within the EC2-Classic network.

AWS Lambda

- AWS Lambda lets you run code without provisioning or managing servers.
- With Lambda, you can run code for virtually any type of application or backend service - all with zero administration.
- Just upload your code and Lambda takes care of everything required to run and scale your code with high availability.

- Just upload your code and Lambda takes care of everything required to run and scale your code with high availability.
- User have no access or control on AWS Lambda infrastructure
- AWS Lambda functions can be configured to run up to 15 minutes per execution.
- ***Serverless computing*** allows you to build and run applications and services without thinking about servers. With serverless computing, your application still runs on servers, but all the server management is done by AWS.
- You can configure triggers to invoke a function in response to resource lifecycle events, respond to incoming HTTP requests, consume events from other AWS Services or AWS Affiliate Services, or run on a schedule. So it's also known as ***Event driven service***
- AWS Lambda natively supports Java, Go, PowerShell, Node.js, C#, Python, and Ruby code, and provides a Runtime API which allows you to use any additional programming languages to author your functions.
- AWS Lambda is priced on a pay per use basis.
- AWS Lambda support versioning.
- You can include your own copy of a library (including the AWS SDK) in order to use a different version than the default one provided by AWS Lambda.

- Lambda functions provide access only to a single VPC.
- There are 3 ways to create lambda function:
  - ☐ **Author from Scratch** - Write on your own function from the scratch
  - ☐ **Use a Blueprint** - Build a Lambda application from sample code and configuration presets for common use case
  - ☐ **Browse serverless app repository** - Deploy a sample lambda application from the AWS Serverless Application Repository

AWS Elastic Beanstalk | FREE

- Elastic Beanstalk is the fastest and simplest way to deploy your application on AWS.
- You can simply upload your code and Elastic Beanstalk automatically handles the deployment, from capacity provisioning, load balancing, auto-scaling to application health monitoring.
- you retain full control over the AWS resources powering your application and can access the underlying resources at any time.
- Easy-to-use service for deploying and scaling web applications and services developed with Java, .NET, PHP, Node.js, Python, Ruby, Go, and Docker on familiar servers such as Apache, Nginx, Passenger, and IIS.

- There is no additional charge for Elastic Beanstalk - you pay only for the AWS resources needed to store and run your applications.
- Choose your platform (Python, Ruby etc.), select Amazon EC2 instance type, select additional services such (RDS, VPC etc) and then upload your code.
- Elastic Beanstalk takes care about provisioning, load balancing, auto scaling and application health monitoring
- You simply use the AWS Management Console, a Git repository, or an integrated development environment (IDE) such as Eclipse or Visual Studio to upload your application

Amazon Lightsail

- Amazon Lightsail is a cost effective, fast and reliable pre-configured Virtual Private Server (VPS).
- Lightsail provides developers compute, storage, and networking capacity and capabilities to deploy and manage websites and web applications in the cloud.
- Lightsail includes everything you need to launch your project quickly – a virtual machine, SSD-based storage, data transfer, DNS management, and a static IP – for a low, predictable monthly price.

- You can get pre configured virtual private server plans that include everything to easily deploy and manage your application.
- Lightsail offers you an easy way to run and scale a wide set of cloud-based applications, at a bundled, predictable, and low price.
- Lightsail is best suited to projects that require a few virtual private servers and users who prefer a simple management interface.
- Common use cases for Lightsail include running websites, web applications, blogs, e-commerce sites, simple software, and more.
- Lightsail console is backed by a publically available API.
- Lightsail block storage provides additional storage volumes (called "attached disks" in Lightsail) that you can attach to your Lightsail instance, similar to an individual hard drive.
- Upgrade to EC2 is a feature that allows you to create a copy of your Lightsail instance in Amazon EC2.
- Lightsail plans are billed on an on-demand hourly rate, so you pay only for what you use.

AWS Outposts

- AWS Outposts delivers fully managed AWS infrastructure, native AWS services, APIs, and tools to virtually any customer on premises facility.

- AWS Outposts enables applications that need to run on premises due to low latency, local data processing, or local data storage needs while removing the undifferentiated heavy lifting required to procure, manage, and upgrade on premises infrastructure.
- Outposts are designed for high availability with redundant top of rack networking switches, power elements, and built-in, always active, additional capacityOutposts are designed for high availability with redundant top of rack networking switches, power elements, and built-in, always active, additional capacity.
- You can use Outposts to securely store and process customer data that needs to remain on premises or in countries where there is no AWS region.
- You can run data intensive workloads on Outposts and process data locally when transmitting data to the cloud is expensive and wasteful and for better control on data analysis, back-up and restore.
- AWS can deliver and install Outposts only in countries where Outposts can be delivered and supported.

EC2 Image Builder | FREE

- EC2 Image Builder simplifies the creation, maintenance, validation, sharing, and deployment of Linux or Windows Server images for use with Amazon EC2 and on-premises.

- With Image Builder, there are no manual steps for updating a server image nor do you have to build your own automation pipeline.
- It integrates with AWS Resource Access Manager and AWS Organizations to enable sharing of automation scripts, recipes, and images across AWS accounts.
- Image Builder is offered at no cost.

CLOUDAI Coffee Break

Send your feedback to us. Your valuable opinion will help CLOUDAI to make continuous improvement of this course

CHAPTER 05 : AWS Storage Services

What are the different AWS Storage Services?

- Amazon Simple Storage Service (S3)
- Amazon Elastic Block Storage (EBS)
- Amazon EC2 Instance Store
- Amazon Elastic File Storage (EFS)
- AWS Storage Gateway

Amazon Simple Storage Service (S3)

- Amazon Simple Storage Service (Amazon S3) is an object storage service that offers industry-leading scalability, data availability, security, and performance.
- Amazon S3 has a simple web services interface that you can use to store and retrieve any amount of data, at any time, from anywhere on the web.
- You can organize your data and configure finely-tuned access controls to meet your specific business, organizational, and compliance requirements.

- Amazon S3 is designed for 99.999999999% (11 9's) of durability, and stores data for millions of applications for companies all around the world.
- Customers of all sizes and industries can use it to store and protect any amount of data for a range of use cases, such as websites, mobile applications, backup and restore, archive, enterprise applications, IoT devices, and big data analytics.
- S3 maintains compliance programs, such as PCI-DSS, HIPAA/HITECH, FedRAMP, EU Data Protection Directive, and FISMA, to help you meet regulatory requirements.
- Store your data in Amazon S3 and secure it from unauthorized access with encryption features and access management tools.
- S3 is the only object storage service that allows you to block public access to all of your objects at the bucket or the account level with S3 Block Public Access.
- S3 integrates with Amazon Macie to discover and protect your sensitive data.
- Amazon Athena to query S3 data with standard SQL expressions
- Amazon Redshift Spectrum to analyze data that is stored across your AWS data warehouses and S3 resources.
- S3 gives you robust capabilities to manage access, cost, replication, and data protection.
- This is a Object storage, NOT Block storage

- In Object storage it stores file and the metadata of the file as a single object and it's key-value paired
- S3 is NOT Region specific, but Bucket is region specific and by default it's the current AWS region.
- There is no storage limit for overall storage volume in S3, but individual object level the maximum storage limit is upto 5 TB
- As much as storage volume you will use the cost will be decreased
- Amazon S3 provides a URL for each and every object it stores and that can be accessed through the internet from any part of the world.
- ***S3 Bucket*** is the Central folder/container in S3, where you store all of your data.
- The S3 Bucket name is unique in the entire AWS namespace.
- Multiple folders can be created under Bucket. It have access control as well
- To upload your data (photos, videos, documents etc.) to Amazon S3, you must first create an S3 bucket in one of the AWS Regions and then then upload any number of objects to the bucket.
- Static websites can be hosted in S3 without connecting to EC2 instances.
- ***Consistency model :*** S3 provides read-after-write consistency for PUTs of new objects and eventual consistency for overwrite PUTs and DELETES

>> Amazon S3 Storage Classes

There are 7 different Storage Classes available in Amazon S3:

1. **S3 Standard** - It delivers low latency and high throughput, S3 Standard is appropriate for a wide variety of use cases, including cloud applications, dynamic websites, content distribution, mobile and gaming applications, and big data analytics.

2. **S3 Intelligent-Tiering** - The S3 Intelligent-Tiering storage class is designed to optimize costs by automatically moving data to the most cost-effective access tier, without performance impact or operational overhead.

   It works by storing objects in two access tiers: one tier that is optimized for frequent access and another lower-cost tier that is optimized for infrequent access.

   Amazon S3 monitors access patterns of the objects in S3 Intelligent-Tiering, and moves the ones that have not been accessed for 30 consecutive days to the infrequent access tier.

   If an object in the infrequent access tier is accessed, it is automatically moved back to the frequent access tier.

   There are no retrieval fees when using the S3 Intelligent-Tiering storage class, and no additional tiering fees when objects are moved between access tiers.

It is the ideal storage class for long-lived data with access patterns that are unknown or unpredictable.

Object Cycle Management: It helps to create to move object from Standard storage to Standard IA and Standard IA to Glacier or define when to delete the object:

- **Transition actions**—Define when objects transition to another storage class. For example, you might choose to transition objects to the S3 Standard-IA storage class 30 days after you created them, or archive objects to the S3 Glacier storage class one year after creating them.
- **Expiration actions**—Define when objects expire. Amazon S3 deletes expired objects on your behalf.

3. **S3 Standard-IA** - S3 Standard-IA is for data that is accessed less frequently, but requires rapid access when needed.

The combination of low cost and high performance make S3 Standard-IA ideal for long-term storage, backups, and as a data store for disaster recovery files.

4. **S3 One Zone-IA** - This is for data that is accessed less frequently, but requires rapid access when needed.

   Unlike other S3 Storage Classes which store data in a minimum of three Availability Zones (AZs), S3 One Zone-IA stores data in a ***single AZ***.

   It's a good choice for storing secondary backup copies of on-premises data or easily recreatable data.

   You can also use it as cost-effective storage for data that is replicated from another AWS Region using S3 ***Cross-Region Replication (CRR).***

   Costs 20% less than S3 Standard-IA.

5. **S3 Glacier** - S3 Glacier is a secure, durable, and low-cost storage class for data archiving.

   You can reliably store any amount of data at costs that are competitive with or cheaper than on-premises solutions.

   S3 Glacier provides three retrieval options that range from a few minutes to hours:
   - **Expedited retrievals :** 1-5 minutes
   - **Standard retrievals :** 3-5 hours
   - **Bulk retrievals :** 5-12 hours

   You can upload objects directly to S3 Glacier, or use S3 Lifecycle policies to transfer data between any of the S3 Storage Classes for active data (S3 Standard, S3 Intelligent-Tiering, S3 Standard-IA, and S3 One Zone-IA) and S3 Glacier.

6.S3 Glacier Deep Archive - S3 Glacier Deep Archive is Amazon S3's lowest-cost storage class and supports long-term retention and digital preservation for data that may be accessed once or twice in a year.

It is designed for customers — particularly those in highly-regulated industries, such as the Financial Services, Healthcare, and Public Sectors — that retain data sets for 7-10 years or longer to meet regulatory compliance requirements.

S3 Glacier Deep Archive can also be used for backup and disaster recovery use cases, and is a cost-effective and easy-to-manage alternative to magnetic tape systems

All objects stored in S3 Glacier Deep Archive are replicated and stored across at least three geographically-dispersed Availability Zones, protected by 99.999999999% of durability, and can be restored within 12 hours.

	S3 Standard	S3 Intelligent-Tiering	S3 Standard-IA	S3 One Zone-IA	S3 Glacier	S3 Glacier Deep Archive
Designed for durability	99.999999999 (11 9's)	99.999999999 (11 9's)	99.999999999 (11 9's)	99.999999999 (11 9's)	99.999999999 (11 9's)	99.999999999 (11 9's)
Designed for availability	99.99%	99.90%	99.90%	99.50%	99.99%	99.99%

Availability SLA	99.90%	99%	99%	99%	99.90%	99.90%
Availability Zones	≥3	≥3	≥3	1	≥3	≥3
Minimum storage duration charge	N/A	30 days	30 days	30 days	90 days	180 days
Retrieval fee	N/A	N/A	per GB retrieved	per GB retrieved	per GB retrieved	per GB retrieved
First byte latency	milliseconds	milliseconds	milliseconds	milliseconds	select minutes or hours	select hours
Storage type	Object	Object	Object	Object	Object	Object
Lifecycle transitions	Yes	Yes	Yes	Yes	Yes	Yes

>> S3 Transfer Acceleration

- Amazon S3 Transfer Acceleration enables fast, easy, and secure transfers of files over long distances between your client and an S3 bucket.
- Transfer Acceleration takes advantage of Amazon CloudFront's globally distributed edge locations.
- As the data arrives at an edge location, data is routed to Amazon S3 over an optimized network path.

- When using Transfer Acceleration, additional data transfer charges may apply.
- Purpose of using S3 Transfer Acceleration:
  - ☐ You have customers that upload to a centralized bucket from all over the world.
  - ☐ You transfer gigabytes to terabytes of data on a regular basis across continents.
  - ☐ You are unable to utilize all of your available bandwidth over the Internet when uploading to Amazon S3.

Amazon Elastic Block Storage (EBS)

- Amazon Elastic Block Store (EBS) is an easy to use, high performance block storage service designed for use with Amazon Elastic Compute Cloud (EC2) for both throughput and transaction intensive workloads at any scale.
- This can be considered as Virtual Hard Disk on the cloud.
- A broad range of workloads, such as relational and non-relational databases, enterprise applications, containerized applications, big data analytics engines, file systems, and media workflows are widely deployed on Amazon EBS.
- You can achieve single digit-millisecond latency for high performance database workloads such as SAP

HANA or gigabyte per second throughput for large, sequential workloads such as Hadoop.

- You can change volume types, tune performance, or increase volume size without disrupting your critical applications, so you have cost-effective storage when you need it.
- Designed for mission-critical systems, EBS volumes are replicated within an Availability Zone (AZ) and can easily scale to petabytes of data.
- One EBS volume can be attached to a single instance but once detached that can be attached to another instance.
- You can use ***EBS Snapshots*** with automated lifecycle policies to back up your volumes in Amazon S3, while ensuring geographic protection of your data and business continuity:

  If you make periodic snapshots of a volume, the snapshots are incremental, which means that only the blocks on the device that have changed after your last snapshot are saved in the new snapshot.
- Even after an Amazon EC2 instance terminates data stored on an Amazon EBS volume can persist independently of the life of the instance.
- EBS encryption enables data at rest security by encrypting your data using Amazon-managed keys, or keys you create and manage using the AWS Key Management Service (KMS).

Amazon EC2 Instance Store

- An instance store provides temporary block-level storage for your instance.
- This storage is located on disks that are physically attached to the host computer.
- Instance stores are ideal for temporary storage of information that changes frequently, such as buffers, caches, scratch data, and other temporary content, or for data that is replicated across a fleet of instances, such as a load-balanced pool of web servers.
- An instance store consists of one or more instance store volumes exposed as block devices.
- You can specify instance store volumes for an instance only when you launch it.
- You can't detach an instance store volume from one instance and attach it to a different instance.
- The data in an instance store persists only during the lifetime of its associated instance.
- If an instance reboots (intentionally or unintentionally), data in the instance store persists.
- In case the underlying disk drive fails, the instance stops, the instance terminates data in the instance store is lost.
- Do not rely on an instance store for valuable, long-term data. Instead, use more durable data storage, such as Amazon S3, Amazon EBS, or Amazon EFS.

Amazon Elastic File Storage (EFS)

- Amazon Elastic File System (Amazon EFS) provides a simple, scalable, fully managed elastic NFS file system for use with AWS Cloud services and on-premises resources.
- It is built to scale on demand to petabytes without disrupting applications, growing and shrinking automatically as you add and remove files, eliminating the need to provision and manage capacity to accommodate growth.
- Amazon EFS offers two storage classes:
    - ☐ Standard storage class
    - ☐ Infrequent Access storage class (EFS IA)
- Amazon EFS is designed to provide massively parallel shared access to thousands of Amazon EC2 instances.
- Amazon EFS is a regional service storing data within and across multiple Availability Zones (AZs) for high availability and durability.
- Amazon EC2 instances can access your file system across AZs, regions, and VPCs, while on-premises servers can access using AWS Direct Connect or AWS VPN.
- Multiple EC2 instances can access an Amazon EFS file system at the same time.
- Amazon EFS is designed to provide performance for a broad spectrum of workloads and applications, including Big Data and analytics, media processing

workflows, content management, web serving, and home directories.

>> When to use Amazon EFS vs EBS vs S3

- Amazon EFS is a file storage service for use with Amazon EC2. Amazon EFS provides a file system interface, file system access semantics (such as strong consistency and file locking), and concurrently-accessible storage for up to thousands of Amazon EC2 instances.

- Amazon EBS is a block level storage service for use with Amazon EC2. Amazon EBS can deliver performance for workloads that require the lowest-latency access to data from a single EC2 instance.

- Amazon S3 is an object storage service. Amazon S3 makes data available through an Internet API that can be accessed anywhere.

AWS Storage Gateway

- AWS Storage Gateway is a hybrid cloud storage service that gives you on-premises access to virtually unlimited cloud storage.

- Customers use Storage Gateway to simplify storage management and reduce costs for key hybrid cloud storage use cases.
- Storage Gateway enables you to reduce your on-premises storage footprint and associated costs by leveraging Amazon S3 cloud storage.
- Useful for moving tape backups to the cloud, reducing on-premises storage with cloud-backed file shares, providing low latency access to data in AWS for on-premises applications, as well as various migration, archiving, processing, and disaster recovery use cases.
- To support these use cases, the service provides three different types of gateways:
    - ☐ **Tape Gateway** - Tape Gateway is a cloud-based Virtual Tape Library (VTL). It presents your backup application with a VTL interface, consisting of a media changer and tape drives. You can create virtual tapes in your virtual tape library using the AWS Management Console. File Gateway presents a file-based interface to
    - ☐ **File Gateway** - Amazon S3, which appears as a network file share. It enables you to store and retrieve Amazon S3 objects through standard file storage protocols.
    - ☐ **Volume Gateway** - Volume Gateway provides an iSCSI target, which enables you to create block storage volumes and mount them as iSCSI devices from your on-premises or EC2

application servers. The Volume Gateway runs in either a cached or stored mode.

CLOUDAI Coffee Break

So far you a good progress and you have covered some of the most important topics. Keep it up

CHAPTER 06: AWS Network & CDN

What are the different AWS Network Services?

- Amazon Virtual Private Cloud (VPC)
- AWS Virtual Private Network (VPN)
- Amazon Route 53
- AWS API Gateway
- AWS Direct Connect
- AWS App Mesh
- AWS Cloud Map
- AWS Global Accelerator
- AWS CloudFront : CDN

Amazon Virtual Private Cloud (VPC)

- Amazon Virtual Private Cloud (Amazon VPC) lets you provision a logically isolated section of the AWS Cloud where you can launch AWS resources in a virtual network that you define.
- You have complete control over your virtual networking environment, including selection of

your own IP address range, creation of subnets, and configuration of route tables and network gateways.

- You can use both IPv4 and IPv6 in your VPC for secure and easy access to resources and applications.
- You can easily customize the network configuration of your Amazon VPC.
- You can also place your backend systems, such as databases or application servers, in a private-facing subnet with no internet access.
- You can use multiple layers of security, including security groups and network access control lists, to help control access to Amazon EC2 instances in each subnet.
- You can store data in Amazon S3 and restrict access so that it's only accessible from instances inside your VPC.
- You can also create dedicated instances that are physically isolated from other AWS accounts, at the hardware level.
- By using Amazon VPC for disaster recovery, you can have all the benefits of a disaster recovery site at a fraction of the cost.
- A default VPC is a logically isolated virtual network in the AWS cloud that is automatically created for your AWS account the first time you provision Amazon EC2 resources.
- You can create other VPCs and use them in addition to your default VPC

- You can have one default VPC in each AWS region.
- If your AWS account has a default VPC, any IAM accounts associated with your AWS account use the same default VPC as your AWS account.
- Move corporate applications to the cloud, launch additional web servers, or add more compute capacity to your network by connecting your VPC to your corporate network.
- You can span a VPC to multiple Availability Zones
- You can run any number of Amazon EC2 instances within a VPC, so long as your VPC is appropriately sized to have an IP address assigned to each instance.
- You can use AMIs in Amazon VPC that are registered within the same region as your VPC.
- You may use Amazon EBS snapshots if they are located in the same region as your VPC.
- You can reserve an instance in Amazon VPC when you purchase Reserved Instances.
- You can use Amazon CloudWatch and Auto Scaling within Amazon VPC.
- ***Peering Connection:*** A peering connection enables you to route traffic via private IP addresses between two peered VPCs.
- ***VPC Endpoints:*** Enables private connectivity to services hosted in AWS, from within your VPC without using an Internet Gateway, VPN, Network Address Translation (NAT) devices, or firewall proxies.

- ***Subnet:*** A segment of a VPC's IP address range where you can place groups of isolated resources.
- ***Internet Gateway:*** The Amazon VPC side of a connection to the public Internet.
- ***Internet Gateway:*** The Amazon VPC side of a connection to the public Internet.
- ***Security groups :*** A security group acts as a virtual firewall for your instance to control inbound and outbound traffic. When you launch an instance in a VPC, you can assign up to five security groups to the instance.
- ***Network ACL :*** A network access control list (ACL) is an optional layer of security for your VPC that acts as a firewall for controlling traffic in and out of one or more subnets.

>> Security groups vs Network ACL

Security groups	Network ACL
Is stateful: Return traffic is automatically allowed, regardless of any rules	Is stateless: Return traffic must be explicitly allowed by rules
Evaluate all rules before deciding whether to allow traffic	Process rules in order, starting with the lowest numbered rule, when deciding whether to allow traffic

Applies to an instance only if someone specifies the security group when launching the instance, or associates the security group with the instance later on	Automatically applies to all instances in the subnets that it's associated with (therefore, it provides an additional layer of defense if the security group rules are too permissive)

AWS Virtual Private Network (VPN)

- AWS Virtual Private Network solutions establish secure connections between your on-premises networks, remote offices, client devices, and the AWS global network.
- AWS VPN is comprised of two services:
    - ☐ AWS Site-to-Site VPN - AWS Site-to-Site VPN creates encrypted tunnels between your network and your Amazon Virtual Private Clouds or AWS Transit Gateways.
    - ☐ AWS Client VPN - AWS Client VPN connects managing remote access of your users to AWS or on-premises resources using a free VPN software client .
- Together, they deliver a highly-available, managed, and elastic cloud VPN solution to protect your network traffic.
- AWS Client VPN provides users with secure access to applications both on premises and in AWS.

- This is particularly helpful during a cloud migration when applications move from on-premises locations to the cloud.
- With AWS Client VPN, users don't have to change the way they access their applications during or after migration.
- The Client VPN endpoint is a regional construct that you configure to use the service.
- A target network is a network that you associate to the Client VPN endpoint that enables secure access to your AWS resources as well as access to on-premises. Currently, the target network is a subnet in your Amazon VPC.
- VPN connection-hours are billed for any time your VPN connections are in the "available" state.

Amazon Route 53

- Amazon Route 53 is a highly available and scalable cloud Domain Name System (DNS) web service.
- It is designed to give developers and businesses an extremely reliable and cost effective way to route end users to Internet applications
- Amazon Route 53 is fully compliant with IPv6
- Amazon Route 53 effectively connects user requests to infrastructure running in AWS – such as Amazon EC2 instances, Elastic Load Balancing load balancers, or Amazon S3 buckets – and can also be

used to route users to infrastructure outside of AWS.

- You can use Amazon Route 53 to configure DNS health checks to route traffic to healthy endpoints or to independently monitor the health of your application and its endpoints.
- Amazon Route 53 offers Domain Name Registration.
- you can purchase and manage domain names and Amazon Route 53 will automatically configure DNS settings for your domains.
- You can also request to transfer in existing domain names from other registrars to be managed by Route 53.
- Route 53 Resolver is a regional DNS service that provides recursive DNS lookups for names hosted in EC2 as well as public names on the internet.
- Private DNS is a Route 53 feature that lets you have authoritative DNS within your VPCs without exposing your DNS records
- DNS Failover consists of two components:
    - ☐ Health checks
    - ☐ Failover
- You can use DNS Failover to maintain a backup site.

Amazon API Gateway

- Amazon API Gateway is an AWS service for creating, publishing, maintaining, monitoring, and securing REST, HTTP, and WebSocket APIs at any scale.
- As an API Gateway API developer, you can create APIs for use in your own client applications.
- You can also make your APIs available to third-party app developers.
- API Gateway supports containerized and serverless workloads, as well as web applications.

AWS Direct Connect

- AWS Direct Connect is a cloud service solution that makes it easy to establish a dedicated network connection from your premises to AWS.
- Using AWS Direct Connect, you can establish private connectivity between AWS and your datacenter, office, or colocation environment
- In many cases can reduce your network costs, increase bandwidth throughput, and provide a more consistent network experience than Internet-based connections.
- AWS Direct Connect lets you establish a dedicated network connection between your network and one of the AWS Direct Connect locations.

- AWS Direct Connect is a network service, and works with all AWS services that are accessible over the Internet, such as Amazon Simple Storage Service (Amazon S3), Elastic Compute Cloud (Amazon EC2), and Amazon Virtual Private Cloud (Amazon VPC).
- AWS Direct Connect Partners can help you extend your pre-existing data center or office network to an AWS Direct Connect location even if your network is not present at an AWS Direct Connect location.
- AWS Direct Connect has two separate charges: port-hours and Data Transfer
- You may transfer any amount of data up to the limit of your selected port capacity.
- ***Link Aggregation Groups (LAG)*** are a way for customers to order and manage multiple direct connect ports as a single larger connection instead of as separate discrete connections.

AWS App Mesh

- AWS App Mesh is a service mesh that provides application-level networking to make it easy for your services to communicate with each other across multiple types of computer infrastructure.
- App Mesh standardizes how your services communicate, giving you end-to-end visibility and ensuring high-availability for your applications.

- AWS App Mesh makes it easy to run services by providing consistent visibility and network traffic controls for services built across multiple types of compute infrastructure.
- App Mesh removes the need to update application code to change how monitoring data is collected or traffic is routed between services.
- App Mesh configures each service to export monitoring data and implements consistent communications control logic across your application.
- This makes it easy to quickly pinpoint the exact location of errors and automatically reroute network traffic when there are failures or when code changes need to be deployed.
- You can use App Mesh with AWS Fargate, Amazon EC2, Amazon ECS, Amazon EKS, and Kubernetes running on AWS, to better run your application at scale.
- App Mesh also integrates with AWS Outposts for your applications running on-premises.

AWS Cloud Map

- AWS Cloud Map is a cloud resource discovery service.

- You can define custom names for your application resources, and it maintains the updated location of these dynamically changing resources.
- This increases your application availability because your web service always discovers the most up-to-date locations of its resources.
- Modern applications are typically composed of multiple services that are accessible over an API and perform a specific function.
- Cloud Map allows you to register any application resources, such as databases, queues, microservices, and other cloud resources, with custom names.

AWS Global Accelerator

- AWS Global Accelerator is a service that improves the availability and performance of your applications with local or global users.
- It provides static IP addresses that act as a fixed entry point to your application endpoints in a single or multiple AWS Regions, such as your Application Load Balancers, Network Load Balancers or Amazon EC2 instances.
- AWS Global Accelerator uses the AWS global network to optimize the path from your users to your applications, improving the performance of your traffic by as much as 60%.

AWS CloudFront : CDN

- Amazon CloudFront is a fast Content Delivery Network (CDN) service that securely delivers data, videos, applications, and APIs to customers globally with low latency, high transfer speeds, all within a developer-friendly environment.
- CloudFront is integrated with AWS – both physical locations that are directly connected to the AWS global infrastructure, as well as other AWS services.
- CloudFront works seamlessly with services including AWS Shield for DDoS mitigation, Amazon S3, Elastic Load Balancing or Amazon EC2 as origins for your applications
- If you use AWS origins such as Amazon S3, Amazon EC2 or Elastic Load Balancing, you don't pay for any data transferred between these services and CloudFront.
- CDN offers a simple, pay-as-you-go pricing model with no upfront fees or required long-term contracts.
- Support for the CDN is included in your existing AWS Support subscription.
- Amazon CloudFront is a highly-secure CDN that provides both network and application level protection.
- With CloudFront, your files are delivered to end-users using a global network of edge locations, which reduces network latency of downloading content from the internet.

- Once any web user accesses content from S3 through CloudFront, it stores in CloudFront and CloudFront distribute that to the Edge locations through Regional Edge locations. It helps users to access the content from the nearest edge location.
- Amazon CloudFront supports delivery of dynamic content that is customized or personalized using HTTP cookies.
- Field-Level Encryption is a feature of CloudFront that allows you to securely upload user-submitted data such as credit card numbers to your origin servers.

CLOUDAI Coffee Break

Work Hard, have fun, make history
- Jeff Bezos

CHAPTER 07 : AWS Database

What are the different AWS Database Services?

- Amazon Relational Database Service (RDS)
- Amazon DynamoDB
- Amazon Redshift
- Amazon DocumentDB
- Amazon Neptune
- Amazon Keyspaces
- Amazon QLDB
- Amazon ElastiCache

Amazon Relational Database Service (RDS)

- Amazon Relational Database Service (Amazon RDS) makes it easy to set up, operate, and scale a relational database in the cloud.
- It provides cost-efficient and resizable capacity while automating time-consuming administration

tasks such as hardware provisioning, database setup, patching and backups.

- It frees you to focus on your applications so you can give them the fast performance, high availability, security and compatibility they need.
- Transactions provide developers atomicity, consistency, isolation, and durability (ACID) across one or more tables within a single AWS account and region.
- Provides you with six familiar database engines:
  - ☐ **Amazon Aurora** - Amazon Aurora is a MySQL and PostgreSQL-compatible relational database built for the cloud, that combines the performance and availability of traditional enterprise databases

    Amazon Aurora is up to five times faster than standard MySQL databases and three times faster than standard PostgreSQL databases.

    Amazon Aurora features a distributed, fault-tolerant, self-healing storage system that auto-scales up to 64TB per database instance.

    It provides the security, availability, and reliability of commercial databases at 1/10th the cost.

    It delivers high performance and availability with up to 15 low-latency read replicas, point-in-time recovery, continuous backup to Amazon S3, and replication across three Availability Zones (AZs).

- ☐ **PostgreSQL** - PostgreSQL has become the preferred open source relational database for many enterprise developers and start-ups, powering leading business and mobile applications.
- ☐ **MySQL** - MySQL is the world's most popular open source relational database and Amazon RDS makes it easy to set up, operate, and scale MySQL deployments in the cloud.
- ☐ **MariaDB** - MariaDB is a popular open source relational database created by the original developers of MySQL.
- ☐ **Oracle Database** - Oracle Database is a relational database management system developed by Oracle.

  You can run Amazon RDS for Oracle under two different licensing models – "License Included" and "Bring-Your-Own-License (BYOL)". In the "License Included" service model, you do not need separately purchased Oracle licenses
- ☐ **SQL Server** - SQL Server is a relational database management system developed by Microsoft.

  Amazon RDS for SQL Server supports the "License Included" licensing model

- You can use the AWS Database Migration Service to easily migrate or replicate your existing databases to Amazon RDS.
- You can run your DB instance in several Availability Zones, an option called a Multi-AZ deployment.
- When you choose Multi-AZ deployment, Amazon automatically provisions and maintains a secondary standby DB instance in a different Availability Zone.
- A security group controls the access to a DB instance.
- You can use the Amazon CloudWatch service to monitor the performance and health of a DB instance.
- You can also subscribe to Amazon RDS events to be notified about changes to a DB instance, DB snapshot, DB parameter group, or DB security group.
- Amazon RDS ***Read Replicas*** provide enhanced performance and durability for RDS database (DB) instances.
- Read Replica make it easy to elastically scale out beyond the capacity constraints of a single DB instance for read-heavy database workloads.
- RDS Supports Vertical scaling with 18 instance sizes for MySQL, PostgreSQL, MariaDB, Oracle, or Microsoft SQL Server instance and 5 instance sizes for Amazon Aurora instance
- RDS also supports Horizontal scaling by unique Domain Name Service (DNS) endpoint to each of

the Read Replicas so that an application can implement load balancing by connecting to the replica endpoint.

Amazon DynamoDB

- Amazon DynamoDB is a fully managed NoSQL database service that provides fast and predictable performance with seamless scalability.
- It's a fully managed, multiregion, multimaster, durable database with built-in security, backup and restore, and in-memory caching for internet-scale applications.
- DynamoDB can handle more than 10 trillion requests per day and can support peaks of more than 20 million requests per second.
- DynamoDB offers encryption at rest, which eliminates the operational burden and complexity involved in protecting sensitive data.
- You can scale up or scale down your tables' throughput capacity without downtime or performance degradation.
- DynamoDB provides on-demand backup capability.
- It allows you to create full backups of your tables for long-term retention and archival for regulatory compliance needs.
- Point-in-time recovery helps protect your tables from accidental write or delete operations.

- With point-in-time recovery, you can restore that table to any point in time during the last 35 days. For more information
- DynamoDB allows you to delete expired items from tables automatically to help you reduce storage usage and the cost of storing data that is no longer relevant.
- Transactions provide developers atomicity, consistency, isolation, and durability (ACID) across one or more tables within a single AWS account and region.
- Amazon DynamoDB auto scaling uses the AWS Application Auto Scaling service to dynamically adjust provisioned throughput capacity on your behalf, in response to actual traffic patterns.
- This enables a table or a global secondary index to increase its provisioned read and write capacity to handle sudden increases in traffic, without throttling.

Amazon Redshift

- Amazon Redshift is a fast, fully managed cloud data warehouse that makes it simple and cost-effective to analyze all your data using standard SQL and your existing Business Intelligence (BI) tools.
- It allows you to run complex analytic queries against terabytes to petabytes of structured data,

using sophisticated query optimization, columnar storage on high-performance storage, and massively parallel query execution.

- Most results come back in seconds.
- Amazon Redshift gives you fast querying capabilities over structured data using familiar SQL-based clients and business intelligence (BI) tools using standard ODBC and JDBC connections.
- Queries are distributed and parallelized across multiple physical resources.
- You can easily scale an Amazon Redshift data warehouse up or down with a few clicks .
- Amazon Redshift automatically patches and backs up your data warehouse, storing the backups for a user-defined retention period.
- AQUA is a new distributed and hardware-accelerated cache that enables Redshift to run up to 10x faster than any other cloud data warehouse.
- When you modify your data warehouse cluster, your requested changes will be applied immediately.

Amazon DocumentDB

- Amazon DocumentDB (with MongoDB compatibility) is a fast, scalable, highly available, and fully managed document database service that supports MongoDB workloads.

- A document database is a type of non relational database that is designed to store and query data as JSON-like documents.
- The flexible, semistructured, and hierarchical nature of documents and document databases allows them to evolve with applications' needs.
- The document model works well with use cases such as catalogs, user profiles, and content management systems where each document is unique and evolves over time.
- Amazon DocumentDB is designed for 99.99% availability and replicates six copies of your data across three AWS Availability Zones (AZs).

Amazon Neptune

- Amazon Neptune is a fast, reliable, fully managed graph database service that makes it easy to build and run applications that work with highly connected datasets.
- Graph databases are purpose-built to store and navigate relationships.
- Amazon Neptune is highly available, with read replicas, point-in-time recovery, continuous backup to Amazon S3, and replication across Availability Zones.
- Neptune is secure with support for HTTPS encrypted client connections and encryption at rest.

Amazon Keyspaces

- Amazon Keyspaces (for Apache Cassandra) is a scalable, highly available, and managed Apache Cassandra–compatible database service.
- With Amazon Keyspaces, you can run your Cassandra workloads on AWS using the same Cassandra application code and developer tools that you use today.
- Amazon Keyspaces gives you the performance, elasticity, and enterprise features you need to operate business-critical Cassandra workloads at scale.

Amazon QLDB

- Amazon QLDB is a fully managed ledger database that provides a transparent, immutable, and cryptographically verifiable transaction log owned by a central trusted authority.
- Data in Amazon QLDB is written to an append-only journal, providing the developer with full data lineage.
- Data in Amazon QLDB's journal is immutable and verifiable, meaning you can trust the data in your ledger.

Amazon ElastiCache

- Amazon ElastiCache allows you to seamlessly set up, run, and scale popular open-Source compatible in-memory data stores in the cloud.
- Build data-intensive apps or boost the performance of your existing databases by retrieving data from high throughput and low latency in-memory data stores.
- Amazon ElastiCache is a popular choice for real-time use cases like Caching, Session Stores, Gaming, Geospatial Services, Real-Time Analytics, and Queuing.
- Amazon ElastiCache offers fully managed Redis and Memcached for your most demanding applications that require sub-millisecond response times:
  - □ **Redis** - Redis, which stands for Remote Dictionary Server, is a fast, open-source, in-memory key-value data store for use as a database, cache, message broker, and queue.

    Redis is a popular choice for caching, session management, gaming, leaderboards, real-time analytics, geospatial, ride-hailing, chat/messaging, media streaming, and pub/sub apps.
  - □ **Memcached** - Memcached is an easy-to-use, high-performance, in-memory data store.

It offers a mature, scalable, open-source solution for delivering sub-millisecond response times making it useful as a cache or session store.

Memcached is a popular choice for powering real-time applications in Web, Mobile Apps, Gaming, Ad-Tech, and E-Commerce.

- Write and memory scaling is supported with sharding.

CLOUDAI Coffee Break

You have completed most of important chapters of Technical sections which is a great achievement and wonder progress. Keep it up....

CHAPTER 08 : AWS Analytics

What are the different AWS Analytics Services?

- Amazon EMR
- AWS Glue
- AWS Data Exchange
- Amazon Athena
- Amazon CloudSearch
- Amazon Elasticsearch Service
- Amazon Kinesis
- AWS Data Pipeline
- AWS Lake Formation
- Amazon MSK

Amazon EMR

- Amazon EMR is the industry-leading cloud big data platform for processing vast amounts of data using open source tools such as Apache Spark, Apache

Hive, Apache HBase, Apache Flink, Apache Hudi, and Presto.

- With EMR you can run Petabyte-scale analysis at less than half of the cost of traditional on-premises solutions and over 3x faster than standard Apache Spark.
- If you have existing on-premises deployments of open source tools such as Apache Spark and Apache Hive, you can also run EMR clusters on ***AWS Outposts.***
- ***EMR Notebooks*** provide a managed environment, based on Jupyter Notebook, that allows data scientists, analysts, and developers to prepare and visualize data, collaborate with peers, build applications, and perform interactive analysis using EMR clusters.

AWS Glue

- AWS Glue is a fully managed extract, transform, and load (ETL) service that makes it easy for customers to prepare and load their data for analytics.
- You can create and run an ETL job with a few clicks in the AWS Management Console.
- AWS Glue consists of a Data Catalog which is a central metadata repository, an ETL engine that can automatically generate Scala or Python code, and a

flexible scheduler that handles dependency resolution, job monitoring, and retries.

- AWS Glue natively supports data stored in Amazon Aurora, Amazon RDS for MySQL, Amazon RDS for Oracle, Amazon RDS for PostgreSQL, Amazon RDS for SQL Server, Amazon Redshift, DynamoDB and Amazon S3, as well as MySQL, Oracle, Microsoft SQL Server, and PostgreSQL databases in your Virtual Private Cloud (Amazon VPC) running on Amazon EC2.
- AWS Glue also supports (in beta) data streams from Amazon MSK, Amazon Kinesis Data Streams, and Apache Kafka.
- The AWS Glue Data Catalog is a central repository to store structural and operational metadata for all your data assets.

AWS Data Exchange

- AWS Data Exchange makes it easy to find, subscribe to, and use third-party data in the cloud.
- AWS Data Exchange makes it easy to reach the millions of AWS customers migrating to the cloud by removing the need to build and maintain infrastructure for data storage, delivery, billing, and entitling.
- Once subscribed to a data product, you can use the AWS Data Exchange API to load data directly into

Amazon S3 and then analyze it with a wide variety of AWS analytics and machine learning services.

- Currently 1,000 data products are available from more than 80 qualified data providers like Change Healthcare, Virtusa, Pitney Bowes, TP ICAP, Vortexa, IMDb, Epsilon, Enigma, TruFactor, ADP are available in AWS Marketplace.

Amazon Athena

- Athena is a serverless query service that makes it easy to analyse large amounts of data stored in Amazon S3 using Standard SQL.
- You simply point Athena at some data stored in Amazon Simple Storage Service (S3), identify your fields, run your queries, and get results in seconds.
- You don't have to build, manage, or tune a cluster or any other infrastructure, and you pay only for the queries that you run.
- Your queries are expressed in standard ANSI SQL and can use JOINs, window functions, and other advanced features.
- Athena is based on the Presto distributed SQL engine and can query data in many different formats including JSON, CSV, log files, text with custom delimiters, Apache Parquet, and Apache ORC.

- Each Athena database can contain one or more tables
- Each Athena table can be comprised of one or more S3 objects

Amazon CloudSearch

- Amazon CloudSearch is a managed service in the AWS Cloud that makes it simple and cost-effective to set up, manage, and scale a search solution for your website or application.
- Amazon CloudSearch supports 34 languages and popular search features such as highlighting, autocomplete, and geospatial search

Amazon Elasticsearch Service

- Amazon Elasticsearch Service is a fully managed service that makes it easy for you to deploy, secure, and run Elasticsearch cost effectively at scale.
- You can build, monitor, and troubleshoot your applications using the tools you love, at the scale you need.
- The service provides support for open source Elasticsearch APIs, managed Kibana, integration with Logstash and other AWS services, and built-in alerting and SQL querying:

- ☐ **Kibana** - Kibana is an open-source data visualization and exploration tool used for log and time-series analytics, application monitoring, and operational intelligence use cases.
- ☐ **Logstash** - Logstash is a light-weight, open-source, server-side data processing pipeline that allows you to collect data from a variety of sources, transform it on the fly, and send it to your desired destination.

Amazon Kinesis

- Amazon Kinesis makes it easy to collect, process, and analyze real-time, streaming data so you can get timely insights and react quickly to new information.
- With Amazon Kinesis, you can ingest real-time data such as video, audio, application logs, website clickstreams, and IoT telemetry data for machine learning, analytics, and other applications.

AWS Data Pipeline

- AWS Data Pipeline, you can regularly access your data where it's stored, transform and process it at scale, and efficiently transfer the results to AWS services such as Amazon S3, Amazon RDS, Amazon DynamoDB, and Amazon EMR.

AWS Data Pipeline

- AWS Lake Formation is a service that makes it easy to set up a secure data lake in days.
- A data lake is a centralized, curated, and secured repository that stores all your data, both in its original form and prepared for analysis.

Amazon MSK

- Amazon MSK is a fully managed service that makes it easy for you to build and run applications that use Apache Kafka to process streaming data.
- Apache Kafka is an open-source platform for building real-time streaming data pipelines and applications.

CLOUDAI Coffee Break

Did you check the latest available date for your test?
It's important to start tracking the exam schedule availability at this point

CHAPTER 09 : AWS Developer Tools

What are the different AWS Development Tools?

- AWS CodeStar
- AWS CodeCommit
- AWS Artifact
- AWS CodeBuild
- AWS CodeDeploy
- AWS CodePipeline
- AWS Cloud9
- AWS X-Ray

AWS CodeStar | FREE

- AWS CodeStar enables you to quickly develop, build, and deploy applications on AWS.
- AWS CodeStar makes it easy for you to set up your entire development and continuous delivery toolchain for coding, building, testing, and deploying your application code.

AWS CodeCommit

- AWS CodeCommit is a secure, highly scalable, managed source ***control service*** that makes it easier for teams to collaborate on code.
- You can use AWS CodeCommit to store anything from code to binaries, and it works seamlessly with your existing Git tools.

AWS Artifact | FREE

- AWS Artifact, available in the console, is a self-service audit artifact retrieval portal that provides our customers with on-demand access to AWS' compliance documentation and AWS agreements.
- It provides on-demand access to AWS' security and compliance reports and select online agreements.
- Reports available in AWS Artifact include our Service Organization Control (SOC) reports, Payment Card Industry (PCI) reports, and certifications from accreditation bodies across geographies and compliance verticals that validate the implementation and operating effectiveness of AWS security controls.

- Agreements available in AWS Artifact include the Business Associate Addendum (BAA) and the Nondisclosure Agreement (NDA).
- Any AWS account has full access on all the agreement documents available in AWS Artifacts.

AWS CodeBuild

- AWS CodeBuild is a fully managed continuous integration service that ***compiles*** source code, ***runs*** tests, and produces software packages that are ready to deploy.
- CodeBuild scales continuously and processes multiple builds concurrently, so your builds are not left waiting in a queue.

AWS CodeDeploy | FREE

- AWS CodeDeploy is a fully managed deployment service that automates software deployments to a variety of ***compute services*** such as Amazon EC2, AWS Fargate, AWS Lambda, and your on-premises servers.
- AWS CodeDeploy makes it easier for you to rapidly release new features, helps you avoid downtime during application deployment, and handles the complexity of updating your applications.

AWS CodePipeline

- AWS CodePipeline automates the ***build, test, and deploy phases*** of your release process every time there is a code change, based on the release model you define.
- You can easily integrate AWS CodePipeline with third-party services such as GitHub or with your own custom plugin.
- AWS CodePipeline integrates with AWS services such as AWS CodeCommit, Amazon S3, AWS CodeBuild, AWS CodeDeploy, AWS Elastic Beanstalk, AWS CloudFormation, AWS OpsWorks, Amazon ECS, and AWS Lambda.

AWS Cloud9

- AWS Cloud9 is a cloud-based integrated development environment (IDE) that lets you write, run, and debug your code with just a browser.
- AWS Cloud9 supports over 40 programming languages, including Node.js (JavaScript), Python, PHP, Ruby, Go, and C++.

AWS X-Ray

- AWS X-Ray helps developers analyze and ***debug production***, distributed applications, such as those built using a microservices architecture.
- With X-Ray, you can understand how your application and its underlying services are performing to identify and troubleshoot the root cause of ***performance issues*** and ***errors***.
- X-Ray provides an end-to-end view of requests as they travel through your application, and shows a map of your application's underlying components.
- You can use X-Ray to analyze both applications in development and in production

CLOUDAI Coffee Break

"Whatever you are, be a good one."
— Abraham Lincoln

CHAPTER 10 : AWS Migration & Transfer

What is the different AWS Migration & Transfer Tools?

- AWS Migration Hub
- AWS Application Discovery Service
- AWS Database Migration Service
- AWS Server Migration Service
- AWS Transfer Family
- AWS Snow Family
- AWS DataSync

AWS Migration Hub | FREE

- AWS Migration Hub provides a single location to track the progress of application migrations across multiple AWS and partner solutions.
- Using Migration Hub allows you to choose the AWS and partner migration tools that best fit your needs, while providing visibility into the status of migrations across your portfolio of applications.

- Migration Hub also provides key metrics and progress for individual applications, regardless of which tools are being used to migrate them.
- Using Migration Hub, you can view the migration progress of all the resources in the application.
- Using Migration Hub, you can view the migration progress of all the resources in the application.
- AWS Migration Hub provides a single place to monitor migrations in any AWS region where your migration tools are available.

AWS Application Discovery Service

- AWS Application Discovery Service helps enterprise customers plan migration projects by gathering information about their on-premises data centers.
- AWS Application Discovery Service collects and presents configuration, usage, and behavior data from your servers to help you better understand your workloads.
- The collected data is retained in encrypted format in an AWS Application Discovery Service data store.
- You can export this data as a CSV file and use it to estimate the Total Cost of Ownership (TCO) of running on AWS and to plan your migration to AWS.
- In addition, this data is also available in AWS Migration Hub, where you can migrate the

discovered servers and track their progress as they get migrated to AWS.

- Once set, the Migration Hub home region cannot be changed.

AWS Database Migration Service

- AWS Database Migration Service helps you migrate databases to AWS quickly and securely.
- The source database remains fully operational during the migration, minimizing downtime to applications that rely on the database.
- The AWS Database Migration Service can migrate your data to and from most widely used commercial and open-source databases.
- AWS Database Migration Service supports homogeneous migrations such as Oracle to Oracle, as well as heterogeneous migrations between different database platforms, such as Oracle or Microsoft SQL Server to Amazon Aurora.
- With AWS Database Migration Service, you can continuously replicate your data with high availability and consolidate databases into a petabyte-scale data warehouse by streaming data to Amazon Redshift and Amazon S3.
- When migrating databases to Amazon Aurora, Amazon Redshift, Amazon DynamoDB or Amazon

DocumentDB (with MongoDB compatibility) you can use DMS free for six months.

AWS Server Migration Service | FREE

- AWS Server Migration Service (SMS) is an agentless service which makes it easier and faster for you to migrate thousands of on-premises workloads to AWS.
- AWS SMS allows you to automate, schedule, and track incremental replications of live server volumes, making it easier for you to coordinate large-scale server migrations.
- Incremental server replication allows you to reduce server downtime significantly.
- Perform migrations faster while minimizing network bandwidth, by migrating only incremental changes made to on-premises servers.
- AWS Server Migration Service is free to use.

AWS Transfer Family

- The AWS Transfer Family provides fully managed support for file transfers directly into and out of Amazon S3.
- With support for Secure File Transfer Protocol (SFTP), File Transfer Protocol over SSL (FTPS), and

File Transfer Protocol (FTP), the AWS Transfer Family helps you seamlessly migrate your file transfer workflows to AWS by integrating with existing authentication systems.

- Additionally by providing DNS routing with Amazon Route 53 so nothing changes for your customers and partners, or their applications.
- With your data in Amazon S3, you can use it with AWS services for processing, analytics, machine learning, and archiving.
- You no longer have to purchase and run your own SFTP, FTPS, or FTP servers and storage to securely exchange data with partners and customers.

AWS Snow Family

- ***AWS Snowball*** is a service that provides secure, rugged devices, so you can bring AWS computing and storage capabilities to your edge environments, and transfer data into and out of AWS.
- Datasets ***less than 10PB*** or distributed in multiple locations, you should use ***Snowball***.
- Those rugged devices are commonly referred to as AWS Snowball or AWS Snowball Edge devices.
- Snowball Edge is an edge computing and data transfer device provided by the AWS Snowball service.

- It has on-board storage and compute power that provides select AWS services for use in edge locations.
- Snowball Edge comes in two options, Storage Optimized and Compute Optimized, to support local data processing and collection in disconnected environments such as ships, windmills, and remote factories.
- Snowball supports specific Amazon EC2 instance types and AWS Lambda functions, so you can develop and test in the AWS Cloud.
- Common use cases include data migration, data transport, image collation, IoT sensor stream capture, and machine learning.
- ***AWS Snowmobile*** is an Exabyte-scale data transfer service used to move extremely large amounts of data to AWS.
- You can transfer up to ***100PB*** per ***Snowmobile***, a 45-foot long ruggedized shipping container, pulled by a semi-trailer truck.
- Snowmobile uses multiple layers of security to help protect your data including dedicated security personnel, GPS tracking, alarm monitoring, 24/7 video surveillance, and an optional escort security vehicle while in transit.
- All data is encrypted with 256-bit encryption keys you manage through the AWS Key Management Service (KMS) and designed for security and full chain-of-custody of your data.

AWS DataSync

- AWS DataSync makes it simple and fast to move large amounts of data online between on-premises storage and Amazon S3, Amazon Elastic File System (Amazon EFS), or Amazon FSx for Windows File Server.
- DataSync can transfer hundreds of terabytes and millions of files at speeds up to 10 times faster than open-source tools, over the internet or AWS Direct Connect links.
- You'll also save on script development and management costs, and avoid the need for costly commercial transfer tools.
- You can move data cost-effectively with DataSync's flat, per-gigabyte pricing.

CLOUDAI Coffee Break

WoW!!!
You have completed 50% of this course. It's recommended to spend some time for a quick recap of the previous chapters

CHAPTER 11 : AWS Management & Governance

What are the different AWS Management & Governance Tools?

- AWS OpsWorks
- AWS Organizations
- AWS Control Tower
- AWS Service Catalog
- AWS License Manager
- AWS Well-Architected Tool
- AWS Trusted Advisor
- AWS Personal Health Dashboard
- AWS CloudFormation
- AWS Config
- AWS CloudWatch
- AWS CloudTrail
- AWS Chatbot
- AWS Launch Wizard
- AWS Systems Manager
- AWS AppConfig

- AWS Compute Optimizer

AWS OpsWorks

- AWS OpsWorks is a configuration management service which automates operations.
- OpsWorks lets you use Chef and Puppet to automate how servers are configured, deployed, and managed across your Amazon EC2 instances or on-premises compute environments.
- Chef and Puppet are automation platforms that allow you to use code to automate the configurations of your servers.
- OpsWorks has three offerings:
    - ☐ AWS Opsworks for Chef Automate
    - ☐ AWS OpsWorks for Puppet Enterprise
    - ☐ OpsWorks Stacks

AWS Organizations | FREE

- AWS Organizations helps you centrally govern your environment as you grow and scale your workloads on AWS.
- Organizations help you to centrally manage billing; control access, compliance, and security; and share resources across your AWS accounts.

- You can automate account creation, create groups of accounts to reflect your business needs, and apply policies for these groups for governance.
- Through integrations with other AWS services, you can use Organizations to define central configurations and resource sharing across accounts in your organization.
- Key components:
  - ☐ **AWS account** - An AWS account is a container for your AWS resources.

    You create and manage your AWS resources in an AWS account, and the AWS account provides administrative capabilities for access and billing.
  - ☐ **Master account** - A master account is the AWS account you use to create your organization.

    From the master account, you can create other accounts in your organization, invite and manage invitations for other accounts to join your organization, and remove accounts from your organization.

    The master account has the role of a payer account and is responsible for paying all charges accrued by the accounts in its organization.

    You can also attach policies to entities such as administrative roots, organizational units (OUs), or accounts within your organization.

You cannot change which account in your organization is the master account.

- ☐ **Member/Linked account** - A member account is an AWS account, other than the master account, that is part of an organization.

  You also can apply policies to member accounts.

  A member account can belong to only one organization at a time.

  But once removed from the existing organization, you can add the member account to another organization.

  You can remove an AWS account that I created using Organizations and make it a standalone account

- ☐ **Administrative root** - An administrative root is the starting point for organizing your AWS accounts.

  The administrative root is the top-most container in your organization's hierarchy.

  Under this root, you can create OUs to logically group your accounts and organize these OUs into a hierarchy that best matches your business needs.

- ☐ **Organizational Unit** - An organizational unit (OU) is a group of AWS accounts within an organization.

  An OU can also contain other OUs enabling you to create a hierarchy. *Example -*

you can group all accounts that belong to the same department into a departmental OU.

OUs are useful when you need to apply the same controls to a subset of accounts in your organization.

Nesting OUs enables smaller units of management. *Example - in a departmental OU, you can group accounts that belong to individual teams in team-level OUs. These OUs inherit the policies from the parent OU in addition to any controls assigned directly to the team-level OU.*

An AWS account can be a member of only one OU at a time.

An OU can be a member of only one OU at a time.

Including root and AWS accounts created in the lowest OUs, your hierarchy can be five levels deep.

- **Policy** - A policy is a "document" with one or more statements that define the controls that you want to apply to a group of AWS accounts.

AWS Organizations supports a specific type of policy called a Service Control Policy (SCP).

An SCP defines the AWS service actions, such as Amazon EC2 RunInstances, that are available for use in different accounts within an organization.

- You can use AWS Organizations to set up a single payment method for all the AWS accounts in your organization through ***consolidated billing***.
- You can use Service Control Policies (SCPs) to apply permission guardrails on AWS Identity and Access Management (IAM) users and roles.

  Example : you can apply an SCP that restricts users in accounts in your organization from launching any resources in regions that you do not explicitly allow.
- You can attach a policies in the following ways:
  - ☐ To the root of your organization (applies to all accounts in your organization)
  - ☐ To individual organizational units (OUs), which applies to all accounts in the OU including nested OUs
  - ☐ To individual accounts
- You can use SCPs to define and enforce the actions that IAM users, groups, and roles can perform in the accounts to which the SCP is applied.
- Principals in a member account (including the root user for the member account) cannot remove or change SCPs that are applied to that account.
- You can not set up multi-factor authentication (MFA) on the AWS account that you have created in your organization programmatically.

- AWS Organizations is available to all AWS customers at no additional charge.

AWS Control Tower | FREE

- Automate the setup of your multi-account AWS environment with just a few clicks.
- AWS Control Tower provides the easiest way to set up and govern a new, secure, multi-account AWS environment based on best practices.
- Control Tower provides you with an integrated dashboard so you can see a top-level summary of policies applied to your AWS environment.
- AWS Control Tower automates the creation of a landing zone with best-practices blueprints that configure AWS Organizations for a multi-account structure.
- AWS Control Tower sets up AWS SSO with a native default directory.
- Customers can use either the Landing Zone solution or AWS Control Tower to create a foundational AWS environment based on best practice blueprints implemented through AWS Service Catalog.
- AWS Control Tower offers an abstracted, automated, and prescriptive experience on top of AWS Organizations.
- It automatically sets up AWS Organizations as the underlying AWS service to organize accounts and

implement preventive guardrails using Service Control Policies (SCPs).

AWS Service Catalog

- Allows organizations to create and manage catalogs of IT services that are approved for use on AWS.
- Allows you to centrally manage commonly deployed IT services.
- These IT services can include everything from virtual machine images, servers, software, and databases to complete multi-tier application architectures.
- Helps you achieve consistent governance and meet your compliance requirements.
- Enable users to quickly deploy only the approved IT services they need.
- End users have a simple portal in which to discover and launch products that comply with organizational policies and budget constraints.
- A portfolio is a collection of products, with configuration information that determines who can use those products and how they can use them.

AWS License Manager | FREE

- Makes it easier to manage your software licenses from software vendors such as Microsoft, SAP, Oracle, and IBM across AWS and on-premises environments.
- Help administrators to create customized licensing rules that emulate the terms of their licensing agreements.
- Enforces these rules when an instance of EC2 gets launched.
- Administrators can use these rules to help prevent licensing violations, such as using more licenses than an agreement stipulates.
- Administrators gain control and visibility of all their licenses with the AWS License Manager dashboard
- Reduce the risk of non-compliance, misreporting, and additional costs due to licensing overages.
- AWS License Manager also simplifies the management of your software licenses that require Amazon EC2 Dedicated Hosts.
- In License Manager, administrators can specify their Dedicated Host management preferences for host allocation and host capacity utilization.

AWS Trusted Advisor | FREE

- It is an application that draws upon best practices learned from AWS' aggregated operational history of serving hundreds of thousands of AWS customers.

- Trusted Advisor inspects your AWS environment and makes recommendations for saving money, improving system performance, or closing security gaps.
- Trusted Advisor includes an ever-expanding list of checks in the following five categories:
  - ☐ **Cost Optimization** – recommendations that can potentially save you money by highlighting unused resources and opportunities to reduce your bill.
  - ☐ **Security** – identification of security settings that could make your AWS solution less secure.
  - ☐ **Fault Tolerance** – recommendations that help increase the resiliency of your AWS solution by highlighting redundancy shortfalls, current service limits, and overutilized resources.
  - ☐ **Performance** – recommendations that can help to improve the speed and responsiveness of your applications.
  - ☐ **Service Limits** – recommendations that will tell you when service usage is more than 80% of the service limit.
- Each customer action in Trusted Advisor triggers an API call that is documented in your Amazon CloudTrail logs.

- Basic and Developer support plan can access only 7 core Trusted Advisor checks.
- Business and Enterprise support plans have access to all Trusted Advisor checks.
- You don't pay anything to use AWS Trusted Advisor.

AWS Personal Health Dashboard | FREE

- It provides alerts and remediation guidance when AWS is experiencing events that may impact you.
- While the ***Service Health Dashboard*** displays the general status of AWS services, Personal Health Dashboard gives you a personalized view into the performance and availability of the AWS services underlying your AWS resources.
- With Personal Health Dashboard, alerts are triggered by changes in the health of AWS resources, giving you event visibility, and guidance to help quickly diagnose and resolve issues.
- AWS Personal Health Dashboard can integrate with Amazon CloudWatch Events.
- Enabling you to build custom rules and select targets such as AWS Lambda functions to define automated remediation actions.
- If you use AWS Organizations, AWS Health allows you to aggregate notifications from all accounts in your organization.

- This allows you to grant or deny access to an AWS Identity and Access Management (IAM) user based on such attributes as event types, event types of a particular service, or other role-based attributes.

AWS CloudFormation | FREE

- It provides a common language for you to model and provision AWS and third party application resources in your cloud environment.
- Allows you to use programming languages or a simple text file to model and provision.
- Codifying your infrastructure allows you to treat your infrastructure as just code.
- Provisions your application resources in a safe, repeatable manner, allowing you to build and rebuild your infrastructure and applications using automation, without having to perform manual actions or write custom scripts.
- AWS CloudFormation supports Elastic Beanstalk application environments.
- There is no additional charge for this service.

AWS Config

- AWS Config is a fully managed service that provides you with an AWS resource inventory, configuration history, and configuration change notifications to enable security and governance.

- You can review changes in configurations and relationships between AWS resources, dive into detailed resource configuration histories.
- Determine your overall compliance against the configurations specified in your internal guidelines.
- Once a change occurs, you are able to quickly review the history of the resource's configuration and determine what the resource's configuration looked like at any point in the past.
- Once change from a previous state is detected, an Amazon Simple Notification Service (SNS) notification can be delivered for you to review and take action.
- Perform configuration audit and compliance verification of both your AWS and third party resources.
- This enables you to simplify compliance auditing, security analysis, change management, and operational troubleshooting.
- The AWS Service Management Connector for Jira Service Desk.

AWS CloudWatch

- Amazon CloudWatch is a monitoring service for AWS cloud resources and the applications you run on AWS.
- It runs on both AWS and on-premises servers.
- You can use Amazon CloudWatch to collect and track metrics, collect and monitor log files, and set alarms.
- Amazon CloudWatch can monitor AWS resources such as Amazon EC2 instances, Amazon DynamoDB tables, and Amazon RDS DB instances, as well as custom metrics generated by your applications and services, and any log files your applications generate.
- You can use Amazon CloudWatch to gain system-wide visibility into resource utilization, application performance, and operational health.
- Amazon CloudWatch can be accessed via API, command-line interface, AWS SDKs, and the AWS Management Console.
- Amazon ***CloudWatch Logs*** lets you monitor and troubleshoot your systems and applications using your existing system, application and custom log files.
- With CloudWatch Logs, you can monitor your logs, in near real time, for specific phrases, values or patterns.

- CloudWatch Logs can ingest, aggregate and monitor any text based common log data or JSON-formatted logs.
- You can retrieve any of your log data using the CloudWatch Logs console or through the CloudWatch Logs CLI.
- Logs Insights introduces a new purpose-built query language for log processing.
- You can create an alarm to monitor any Amazon CloudWatch metric in your account.
- Alarm history is available for 14 days.
- Amazon CloudWatch Dashboards allow you to create, customize, interact with, and save graphs of AWS resources and custom metrics.
- The CloudWatch home page automatically displays metrics about every AWS service you use.
- You can additionally create custom dashboards to display metrics about your custom applications, and display custom collections of metrics that you choose.
- Dashboards will auto refresh while you have them open.
- Amazon CloudWatch Events (CWE) is a stream of system events describing changes in your AWS resources.
- Currently, Amazon EC2, Auto Scaling, and AWS CloudTrail are supported.

- CloudWatch Container Insights is a feature for monitoring, troubleshooting, and alarming on your containerized applications and microservices.
- You use Amazon SNS with CloudWatch to send messages when an alarm threshold has been reached.
- When CloudTrail logging is turned on, CloudWatch writes log files to the Amazon S3 bucket that you specified when you configured CloudTrail.

AWS CloudTrail | FREE

- AWS CloudTrail is a web service that records activity made on your account and delivers log files to your Amazon S3 bucket.
- CloudTrail records important information about each action, including who made the request, the services used, the actions performed, parameters for the actions, and the response elements returned by the AWS service.
- This information helps you to track changes made to your AWS resources and to troubleshoot operational issues.
- CloudTrail makes it easier to ensure compliance with internal policies and regulatory standards.
- You can easily view recent events in the CloudTrail console by going to Event history.

- AWS CloudTrail will only show the results of the CloudTrail Event History for the current region you are viewing for the last 90 days.
- By default, log files are stored in S3 bucket indefinitely, but you control the retention policies for your CloudTrail log files.
- CloudTrail delivers log files to your S3 bucket approximately every 5 minutes.
- CloudTrail logs in S3 bucket can be encrypted using AWS Key Management Service (KMS).
- AWS CloudTrail is free, but once a CloudTrail trail is set up, Amazon S3 charges apply based on your usage.

AWS Chatbot | FREE

- AWS Chatbot is an interactive agent that makes it easy to monitor and interact with your AWS resources in your Slack channels and Amazon Chime chat rooms.
- With AWS Chatbot you can receive alerts, run commands to return diagnostic information, invoke AWS Lambda functions, and create AWS support cases.

AWS Launch Wizard | FREE

- AWS Launch Wizard offers a guided way of sizing, configuring, and deploying AWS resources for third party applications, such as Microsoft SQL Server Always On and HANA based SAP systems, without the need to manually identify and provision individual AWS resources.
- There is no additional cost to use this service.

AWS Systems Manager

- Systems Manager provides a unified user interface so you can view operational data from multiple AWS services and allows you to automate operational tasks across your AWS resources.
- With Systems Manager, you can group resources, like Amazon EC2 instances, Amazon S3 buckets, or Amazon RDS instances, by application, view operational data for monitoring and troubleshooting, and take action on your groups of resources.

AWS AppConfig

- Use AWS AppConfig, a capability of AWS Systems Manager, to create, manage, and quickly deploy application configurations.

- AppConfig supports controlled deployments to applications of any size and includes built-in validation checks and monitoring.
- You can use AppConfig with applications hosted on EC2 instances, AWS Lambda, containers, mobile applications, or IoT devices.

AWS Compute Optimizer | FREE

- AWS Compute Optimizer recommends optimal AWS Compute resources for your workloads to reduce costs and improve performance by using machine learning to analyze historical utilization metrics.
- There is no additional change for this service.

CLOUDAI Coffee Break

"You never fail until you stop trying."

- Albert Einstein

CHAPTER 12 : AWS Application Integration

What are the different AWS Application Integration Tools?

- AWS Simple Notification Service (SNS)
- AWS Simple Queue Service (SQS)
- Amazon Step Function
- Amazon AppFlow
- Amazon EventBridge
- Amazon MQ
- Amazon SWF

AWS Simple Notification Service (SNS)

- Amazon Simple Notification Service (Amazon SNS) is a web service that makes it easy to set up, operate, and send notifications from the cloud.
- It provides developers with a highly scalable, flexible, and cost-effective capability to publish messages from an application and immediately deliver them to subscribers or other applications.
- Amazon SNS follows the "publish-subscribe" (pub-sub) messaging paradigm, with notifications being delivered to clients using a "push" mechanism that eliminates the need to periodically check or "poll" for new information and updates.
- Simple APIs and easy integration with applications.
- Inexpensive, pay-as-you-go model with no up-front costs.

- Your publisher systems can fan out messages to a large number of subscriber endpoints for parallel processing, including Amazon SQS queues, AWS Lambda functions, and HTTP/S webhooks.
- SNS can be used to fan out notifications to end users using mobile push, SMS, and email.
- Amazon CloudWatch uses Amazon SNS to send email. First, create and subscribe to an SNS topic.
- Amazon SNS topic owners can keep sensitive data secure by setting topic policies that restrict who can publish and subscribe to a topic.
- Amazon SNS leverages the proven AWS cloud to dynamically scale with your application.
- Amazon SNS uses cross availability zone message storage to provide high message durability.

AWS Simple Queue Service (SQS)

- Amazon Simple Queue Service (SQS) is a fully managed message queuing service that enables you to decouple and scale microservices, distributed systems, and serverless applications.
- SQS eliminates the complexity and overhead associated with managing and operating message oriented middleware.
- You can send, store, and receive messages between software components at any volume, without losing messages or requiring other services to be available.

- SQS FIFO queues are designed to guarantee that messages are processed exactly once, in the exact order that they are sent.
- Amazon SQS works on a massive scale, processing billions of messages per day.
- You can scale the amount of traffic you send to Amazon SQS up or down without any configuration.
- Amazon SQS provides message ordering. FIFO (first-in-first-out) queues preserve the exact order in which messages are sent and received.
- FIFO queues provide exactly-once processing, which means that each message is delivered once and remains available until a consumer processes it and deletes it. Duplicates are not introduced into the queue.
- SQS offers two types of message queues:
  - ☐ Standard queues
  - ☐ SQS FIFO queues

Amazon Step Functions

- AWS Step Functions lets you coordinate multiple AWS services into serverless workflows so you can build and update apps quickly.
- Workflows are made up of a series of steps, with the output of one step acting as input into the next.

- Application development is simpler and more intuitive using Step Functions, because it translates your workflow into a state machine diagram that is easy to understand, easy to explain to others, and easy to change.
- Step Functions automatically triggers and tracks each step, and retries when there are errors, so your application executes in order and as expected.

Amazon AppFlow

- Amazon AppFlow is a fully managed integration service that enables you to securely transfer data between Software-as-a-Service (SaaS) applications like Salesforce, Marketo, Slack, and ServiceNow, and AWS services like Amazon S3 and Amazon Redshift, in just a few clicks.

Amazon EventBridge

- Amazon EventBridge is a serverless event bus that makes it easy to connect applications together using data from your own applications, integrated Software-as-a-Service (SaaS) applications, and AWS services.
- EventBridge makes it easy to build event-driven applications .

Amazon MQ

- Amazon MQ is a managed message broker service for Apache ActiveMQ that makes it easy to set up and operate message brokers in the cloud.

Amazon SWF

- Amazon Simple Workflow Service (SWF) helps developers build, run, and scale background jobs that have parallel or sequential steps.

CLOUDAI Coffee Break

The next 2 chapters are on AWS Security. 25% of the examination will come from this section.
So be focused....

CHAPTER 13 : AWS Identity and IAM

What are the different AWS Security, Identity & Compliance Tools?

- AWS Identity and Access Management (IAM)
- Manage IAM credentials
- Root User
- IAM Users
- IAM Groups
- IAM Roles
- IAM Policies

AWS Identity and Access Management (IAM) | FREE

- AWS Identity and Access Management (IAM) is a web service that helps you securely control access to AWS resources.
- You use IAM to control who is authenticated (signed in) and authorized (has permissions) to use resources.

- Using IAM, you can create and manage AWS users and groups, and use permissions to allow and deny their access to AWS resources.
- You can also use IAM for the users outside AWS.
- ***Shared access*** - You can grant other people permission to administer and use resources in your AWS account without having to share your password or access key.
- ***Granular permissions*** - You can grant different permissions to different people for different resources.
- ***Identity federation*** - You can allow users who already have passwords elsewhere.

  Example - In your corporate network (Active Directory) or with an internet identity provider—to get temporary access to your AWS account.
- ***Identity information for assurance*** - If you use AWS CloudTrail, you receive log records that include information about those who made requests for resources in your account.

  That information is based on IAM identities.
- ***PCI DSS Compliance*** - IAM supports the processing, storage, and transmission of credit card data by a merchant or service provider, and has been validated as being compliant with Payment Card Industry (PCI) Data Security Standard (DSS).
- ***Eventually Consistent*** - IAM achieves high availability by replicating data across multiple

servers within Amazon's data centers around the world.

Any changes must be replicated across IAM, which can take some time.

- You can use IAM features to securely provide credentials for applications that run on EC2 instances.

  These credentials provide permissions for your application to access other AWS resources.
- IAM can be used to grant your employees and applications federated access to the AWS Management Console and AWS service APIs, using your existing identity systems such as Microsoft Active Directory (AD).
- By default IAM users have only login permission with no additional access.
- You can not use IAM for application level authentication.
- IAM power users have all the access like Admin users except creating and managing IAM users and Groups.
- IAM is a feature of your AWS account offered at no additional charge.

Manage IAM credentials

- **Passwords** - IAM users who use the AWS Management Console to work with AWS resources must have a password in order to sign in.

  You can create, change, or delete a password for your Root user or an IAM user in your AWS account.

  After you have assigned a password to a user, the user can sign in to the AWS Management Console using the sign-in URL

  In addition to manually creating individual passwords for your IAM users, you can create a password policy that applies to all IAM user passwords in your AWS account.

  Even if your users have their own passwords, they still need permissions to access your AWS resources.

  You can use a password policy to do these things:

  - ☐ Set a minimum password length.
  - ☐ Require specific character types, including uppercase letters, lowercase letters, numbers, and non-alphanumeric characters.
  - ☐ Allow all IAM users to change their own passwords.
  - ☐ Require IAM users to change their password after a specified period of time (enable password expiration).

- ☐ Prevent IAM users from reusing previous passwords.
- ☐ Force IAM users to contact an account administrator when the user has allowed his or her password to expire.

- **Access keys** - Access keys are long-term credentials for an IAM user or the AWS account root user.

  Access keys consist of two parts:

  - ☐ Access key ID
  - ☐ Secret access key

  Used to make programmatic calls to AWS from the AWS APIs, AWS CLI, AWS SDKs, or AWS Tools for Windows PowerShell.

  You are limited to two access keys for each IAM user, which is useful when you want to rotate the access keys.

  As a best practice, use temporary security credentials (IAM roles) instead of access keys, and disable any AWS account root user access keys.

  When you create an access key pair, save the access key ID and secret access key in a secure location.

  The secret access key is available only at the time you create it.

  If you lose your secret access key, you must delete the access key and create a new one.

You can also create and use temporary access keys, known as ***temporary security credentials***.

- **Key pairs** - Key pairs are unrelated to access keys, and consist of a public key and a private key.

  You use the private key to create a digital signature, and then AWS uses the corresponding public key to validate the signature.

  AWS does not provide key pairs for your account; you must create them.

  Key pairs are used only the following services :

  - ☐ **Amazon EC2** - You can create Amazon EC2 key pairs from the Amazon EC2 console, CLI, or API.
  - ☐ **Amazon CloudFront** - You create Amazon CloudFront key pairs from the Security Credentials.

    Only the AWS account root user (not IAM users) can create CloudFront key pairs.

- **SSH public keys** - Used to authenticate to AWS CodeCommit repositories.

  There are two ways to register a user's public SSH key:

  - ☐ An administrative user can assign a public SSH key to one or more users and provide them with the corresponding private key.

☐ An administrative user can enable self-management for one or more users.

- **Multi-Factor Authentication (MFA)** - AWS Multi-Factor Authentication (MFA) is a simple best practice that adds an extra layer of protection on top of your user name and password.

  With MFA enabled, when a user signs in to an AWS Management Console, they will be prompted for their username and password (the first factor—what they know), as well as for an authentication code from their AWS MFA device (the second factor—what they have).

  Taken together, these multiple factors provide increased security for your AWS account settings and resources.

  You can enable MFA for your AWS account and for individual IAM users you have created under your account.

  MFA can also be used to control access to AWS service APIs.

  You can also protect cross-account access using MFA.

- **Server Certificates** - To enable HTTPS connections to your website or application in AWS, you need an SSL/TLS server certificate.

  For certificates in a Region supported by AWS Certificate Manager (ACM), we recommend that you use ACM to provision, manage, and deploy your server certificates.

In unsupported Regions, you must use IAM as a certificate manager.

Use IAM as a certificate manager only when you must support HTTPS connections in a Region that is not supported by ACM.

ACM is the preferred tool to provision, manage, and deploy your server certificates.

Root User

- When you first create an Amazon Web Services (AWS) account, you begin with a single sign-in identity that has complete access to all AWS services and resources in the account called Root User.
- Amazon recommends NOT to use the Root User account for daily activity, rather it's advisable to create an IAM User with Administrative privilege to manage administrative work for the account.
- Root User is accessed by signing in with the email address and password that you used to create the account.
- You can create, rotate, disable, or delete access keys (access key IDs and secret access keys) for your AWS account root user.
- You can also change your root user password.

- Anyone who has root user credentials for your AWS account has unrestricted access to all the resources in your account, including billing information.
- When you create access keys, you create the access key ID and secret access key as a set.
- During access key creation, AWS gives you one opportunity to view and download the secret access key part of the access key.
- If you don't download it or if you lose it, you can delete the access key and then create a new one.
- You can create root user access keys with the IAM console, AWS CLI, or AWS API.
- You are limited to two access keys for each IAM user, which is useful when you want to rotate the access keys.
- You can also assign up to two access keys to the root user.
- When you disable an access key, you can't use it for API calls, and inactive keys do count toward your limit.
- You can create or delete an access key any time.
- However, when you delete an access key, it's gone forever and can't be retrieved.
- Root User allow the following MFA :
    - ☐ Virtual MFA device
    - ☐ Hardware MFA device

IAM Users

- An AWS Identity and Access Management (IAM) user is an entity that you create in AWS to represent the person or application that uses it to interact with AWS.
- A user in AWS consists of a name and credentials.
- An IAM user with administrator permissions is different from the AWS account root user.
- Administrators have the highest privileges within IAM user access.
- When you create a user, IAM creates these ways to identify that user:
  - ☐ A "friendly name" for the user, which is the name that you specified when you created the user.
  - ☐ An Amazon Resource Name (ARN) for the user. You use the ARN when you need to uniquely identify the user across all of AWS.
  - ☐ A unique identifier for the user. This ID is returned only when you use the API, Tools for Windows PowerShell, or AWS CLI to create the user.

    You do not see this ID in the console.
- ***Console password*** - A password that the user can type to sign in to interactive sessions such as the AWS Management Console.
- ***Access keys*** - A combination of an access key ID and a secret access key.

These can be used to make programmatic calls to AWS.

You can assign two to a user at a time.

- ***SSH keys for use with CodeCommit:*** An SSH public key in the OpenSSH format that can be used to authenticate with CodeCommit.
- ***Server certificates:*** SSL/TLS certificates that you can use to authenticate with some AWS services.
- Create and change the passwords that permit access to the AWS Management Console.
- Set a password policy to enforce a minimum password complexity.
- Allow users to change their own passwords.
- Create and update access keys for programmatic access to the resources in your account.
- You can enhance the security of the user's credentials by enabling multi-factor authentication (MFA) for the user.
- The security best practice is to remove passwords and access keys when users no longer need them.
- You can generate and download a credential report that lists all IAM users in your account and the status of their various credentials, including passwords, access keys, and MFA devices.
- The credential report shows how recently the password or access key has been used.
- Each IAM user is associated with one and only one AWS account.

- Since users are defined within your AWS account, they don't need to have a payment method on file with AWS.
- Any AWS activity performed by users in your account is billed to your account.
- The number and size of IAM resources in an AWS account are limited.
- By default, a brand new IAM user has no permissions to do anything like to perform any AWS operations or to access any AWS resources.
- An advantage of having individual IAM users is that you can assign permissions individually to each user.
- You might assign administrative permissions to a few users, who then can administer your AWS resources and can even create and manage other IAM users.
- In most cases, however, you want to limit a user's permissions to just the tasks (AWS actions or operations) and resources that are needed for the job.
- You can also add a permissions boundary to your users.
- ***Users as service accounts*** - An IAM user can represent a person or an application that uses its credentials to make AWS requests. service account, referred to as a service account.

If you choose to use the long-term credentials of an IAM user in your application, do not embed access keys directly into your application code.

The AWS SDKs and the AWS Command Line Interface allow you to put access keys in known locations so that you do not have to keep them in code.

IAM Groups

- An IAM group is a collection of IAM users.
- Groups let you specify permissions for multiple users, which can make it easier to manage the permissions for those users.
- You can create a group with required permissions for a specific team and add any new member joining into the team which will automatically provide all the defined access to the new user.
- A group is not truly an "identity" in IAM because it cannot be identified as a Principal in a permission policy.
- It is simply a way to attach policies to multiple users at one time.
- A group can contain many users, and a user can belong to multiple groups.
- Groups can't be nested; they can contain only users, not other groups.

- There's no default group that automatically includes all users in the AWS account.
- If you want to have a group like that, you need to create it and assign each new user to it.
- The number and size of IAM resources in an AWS account are limited.

IAM Roles

- An IAM role is an IAM identity that you can create in your account that has specific permissions.
- An IAM role is similar to an IAM user, in that it is an AWS identity with permission policies that determine what the identity can and cannot do in AWS.
- However, instead of being uniquely associated with one person, a role is intended to be assumable by anyone who needs it.
- You can use roles to delegate access to users, applications, or services that don't normally have access to your AWS resources.
- You can delegate access to AWS resources using an IAM role.
- A role does not have standard long-term credentials such as a password or access keys associated with it.
- Instead, when you assume a role, it provides you with temporary security credentials for your role session.

- You can use IAM tags to add custom attributes to an IAM entity (user or role) using a tag key–value pair.
- You can use the AWS Security Token Service (AWS STS) to create and provide trusted users with temporary security credentials that can control access to your AWS resources.
- ***Temporary security credentials*** work almost identically to the long-term access key credentials that your IAM users can use, with the following differences:
    - ☐ They can be configured to last for anywhere from a few minutes to several hours.
    - ☐ Temporary security credentials are not stored with the user but are generated dynamically and provided to the user when requested.
- IAMA Roles for Amazon EC2 - Amazon EC2 uses an instance profile as a container for an IAM role.

  An instance profile can contain only one IAM role and this limit can't be increased.

  Using IAM roles applications can securely make API requests from your instances, without requiring you to manage the security credentials that the applications use.
- ***Identity Providers and Federation (IdP)*** - If you already manage user identities outside of AWS, you can use IAM identity providers instead of creating IAM users in your AWS account.

When you use an IAM identity provider, you don't have to create custom sign-in code or manage your own user identities. The IdP provides that for you.

Your external users sign in through a well-known IdP, such as Login with Amazon, Facebook, or Google.

You can give those external identities permissions to use AWS resources in your account.

IAM supports IdPs that are compatible with OpenID Connect (OIDC) or SAML 2.0 (Security Assertion Markup Language 2.0)

- You can use IAM roles to delegate access to your AWS resources.
- A ***service-linked role*** is a unique type of IAM role that is linked directly to an AWS service.

IAM Policies

- A policy is an entity that, when attached to an identity or resource, defines their permissions.
- You can use the AWS Management Console, AWS CLI, or AWS API to create customer managed policies in IAM.
- ***Customer managed policies*** are standalone policies that you administer in your own AWS account and grant permissions to an identity.

You can then attach the policies to identities (users, groups, and roles) in your AWS account.

- AWS supports **six** types of policies:
  - ☐ **Identity-based policies** - A policy that is attached to an identity in IAM is known as an identity-based policy.

    Identity-based policies can include:
    - **AWS managed policies** - AWS managed policies are created and managed by AWS where you can use them, but you can't manage them.

      AWS managed policies usually provide broad administrative or read-only permissions.
    - **Inline policies** - An inline policy is one that you create and embed directly to an IAM group, user, or role. Inline policies can't be reused on other identities or managed outside of the identity where it exists.
    - **Customer managed policies** - Provide more precise control over your policies than AWS managed policies. You can create and edit an IAM policy in the visual editor or by creating the JSON policy document directly.
  - ☐ **Resource-based policies** - Attach inline policies to resources.

- ☐ **Permissions boundaries** - That policy defines the maximum permissions that the identity-based policies can grant to an entity, but does not grant permissions.
- ☐ **Organizations SCPs** - Use an AWS Organizations service control policy (SCP) to define the maximum permissions for account members of an organization or organizational unit (OU).
- ☐ **ACLs** - ACLs are cross-account permissions policies that grant permissions to the specified principal.

  ACLs are similar to resource-based policies, although they are the only policy type that does not use the JSON policy document structure.
- ☐ **Session policies** - Session policies limit the permissions that the role or user's identity-based policies grant to the session.

- As a best practice, use customer managed policies instead of inline policies.
- It's also best to use customer managed policies instead of AWS managed policies.
- You cannot attach identity-based policies to the root user, and you cannot set the permissions boundary for the root user.
- However, you can specify the root user as the principal in a resource-based policy or an ACL

- As a member of an account, the root user is affected by any SCPs for the account.
- You can use the AWS Management Console, AWS CLI, or AWS API to create customer managed policies in IAM.
- Most policies are stored in AWS as JSON documents.

CHAPTER 14 : AWS Security & Compliance

What are the different AWS Security & Compliance Tools?

- AWS Resource Access Manager (RAM)
- Amazon Cognito
- Amazon GuardDuty
- Amazon Macie
- AWS Inspector
- AWS Directory Service
- AWS Single Sign-On (SSO)
- AWS Key Management Service (KMS)
- AWS CloudHSM
- AWS Secrets Manager
- AWS Certificate Manager
- AWS Firewall Manager
- AWS Web Application Firewall (WAF)
- AWS Shield
- AWS Security Hub
- Amazon Detective
- AWS Artifact

AWS Resource Access Manager (RAM) | FREE

- This service enables you to easily and securely share AWS resources with any AWS account or within your AWS Organization.
- You can create resources centrally in a multi-account environment and share them across the accounts.
- RAM leverages existing policies and permissions set in AWS Identity and Access Management (IAM) to govern the consumption of shared resources.
- Sharing resources such as AWS License Manager configurations across accounts allows you to leverage licenses in multiple parts of your company to increase utilization and optimize costs.
- RAM also provides comprehensive visibility into shared resources to set alarms and visualize logs through integration with Amazon CloudWatch and AWS CloudTrail.
- Sharable resources - AWS App Mesh, Amazon Aurora, AWS CodeBuild, Amazon EC2, Amazon EC2 Image Builder, AWS License Manager, AWS Resource Groups, Amazon Route 53

AWS Resource

- Amazon Cognito lets you add user sign-up, sign-in, and access control to your web and mobile apps quickly and easily.
- It scales to millions of users and supports sign-in with social identity providers, such as Facebook, Google, and Amazon, and enterprise identity providers via SAML 2.0.
- Amazon Cognito supports multi-factor authentication and encryption of data-at-rest and in-transit.
- Amazon Cognito is HIPAA eligible and PCI DSS, SOC, ISO/IEC 27001, ISO/IEC 27017, ISO/IEC 27018, and ISO 9001 compliant.

Amazon GuardDuty

- Amazon GuardDuty is a threat detection service that continuously monitors for malicious activity and unauthorized behavior to protect your AWS accounts and workloads.
- The service uses machine learning, anomaly detection, and integrated threat intelligence to identify and prioritize potential threats.
- It operates completely independently from your resources so there is no risk of performance or availability impacts to your workloads.

- GuardDuty analyzes tens of billions of events across multiple AWS data sources, such as AWS CloudTrail, Amazon VPC Flow Logs, and DNS logs.
- By integrating with Amazon CloudWatch Events, Amazon GuardDuty delivers detailed and actionable alerts that are easy to integrate with existing event management and workflow systems.
- Provides multi account support , that let you manage all of your AWS accounts from a centralized security account

Amazon Macie

- Amazon Macie is a fully managed data security and data privacy service that uses machine learning and pattern matching to discover and protect your sensitive data in AWS.
- Macie automatically detects a large and growing list of sensitive data types, including personally identifiable information (PII) such as names, addresses, and credit card numbers.
- It also gives you constant visibility of the data security and data privacy of your data stored in Amazon S3 using Machine Learning.
- Macie's alerts or findings, can be searched and filtered in the AWS Management Console and sent to Amazon CloudWatch Events for easy integration with existing workflow or event management

systems, or to be used in combination with AWS services, such as AWS Step Functions to take automated remediation actions.

- This can help you meet regulations, such as the Health Insurance Portability and Accountability Act (HIPAA) and General Data Privacy Regulation (GDPR).
- Macie provides multi-account support using AWS Organizations.

>> Amazon GuardDuty vs Amazon Macie

Amazon GuardDuty	Amazon Macie
Provides broad protection of your AWS accounts, workloads, and data by helping to identify threats such as attacker reconnaissance, instance compromise, and account compromise.	Helps you protect your data in Amazon S3 by helping you classify what data you have, the value that data has to the business, and the behavior associated with access to that data.

AWS Inspector

- This is an automated security assessment service that helps improve the security and compliance of applications deployed on AWS.

- There is no performance impact to your application when running an agentless assessment with the network reachability rules package, but minimal performance impact during the data collection phase.
- Amazon Inspector automatically assesses applications for exposure, vulnerabilities, and deviations from best practices.
- Once assessment is done, Amazon Inspector produces a detailed list of security findings prioritized by level of severity.
- Amazon Inspector security assessments help you check for unintended network accessibility of your Amazon EC2 instances and for vulnerabilities on those EC2 instances.

AWS Directory Service

- AWS Directory Service for Microsoft Active Directory, also known as AWS Managed Microsoft AD, enables your directory-aware workloads and AWS resources to use managed Active Directory in the AWS Cloud.
- AWS Managed Microsoft AD is built on the actual Microsoft Active Directory and does not require you to synchronize or replicate data from your existing Active Directory to the cloud.

- Provide directories that contain information about your organization, including users, groups, computers, and other resources.
- Helpful to implement group level user or application rules throughout the organization.
- You can use standard Active Directory administration tools and take advantage of built-in Active Directory features, such as Group Policy and single sign-on (SSO).
- With AWS Managed Microsoft AD, you can easily join Amazon EC2 and Amazon RDS for SQL Server instances to your domain, and use AWS Enterprise IT applications such as Amazon WorkSpaces with Active Directory users and groups.
- AWS Managed Microsoft AD makes it easy to migrate Active Directory–dependent applications and Windows workloads to the AWS Cloud.
- There are several third party software such as Azure Active Directory (Azure AD), Office 365, Microsoft SharePoint Server, Distributed File System Replication (DFSR) and many more are compatible with AWS Directory Service.

AWS Single Sign-On (SSO) | FREE

- AWS Single Sign-On (SSO) makes it easy to centrally manage access to multiple AWS accounts and business applications and provide users with single sign-on access to all their assigned accounts and applications from one place.

- Eliminate the need of managing and remembering multiple passwords for multiple applications within your organization.
- Easily manage access and user permissions to all of your accounts in AWS Organizations centrally.
- AWS SSO also includes built-in integrations to many business applications, such as Salesforce, Box, and Office 365.
- Using AWS SSO, you can create and manage user identities in AWS SSO's identity store, or easily connect to your existing identity source including Microsoft Active Directory, Azure Active Directory (Azure AD), and Okta Universal Directory.
- You can connect AWS SSO to your existing identity source and configure permissions that grant your users access to their assigned AWS Organizations accounts and hundreds of pre-integrated cloud applications, all from a single user portal.
- All administrative and sign-in activity is recorded in AWS CloudTrail, helping you meet your audit and compliance requirements.
- You can centrally view when users attempt to access accounts and applications, including from what IP address.
- AWS SSO is offered at no extra charge.

AWS Key Management Service (KMS)

- AWS KMS is a managed service that enables you to easily create and control the keys used for cryptographic operations.
- The service provides a highly available key generation, storage, management, and auditing solution for you to encrypt or digitally sign data within your own applications or control the encryption of data across AWS services.
- AWS KMS is integrated with AWS CloudTrail to provide you with logs of all key usage to help meet your regulatory and compliance needs.
- AWS KMS is supported in AWS SDKs, AWS Encryption SDK, the Amazon DynamoDB Client-side Encryption, and the Amazon S3 Encryption Client to facilitate encryption of data within your own applications wherever they run.
- You can import a copy of your key from your own key management infrastructure to AWS KMS and use it with any integrated AWS service or from within your own applications.
- You cannot import asymmetric CMKs into AWS KMS.
- You can choose to have AWS KMS automatically rotate CMKs every year, provided that those keys were generated within AWS KMS HSMs.
- The security and quality controls in AWS KMS have been certified under multiple compliance schemes to simplify your own compliance obligations.

AWS CloudHSM

- AWS CloudHSM is a cloud-based hardware security module (HSM) that enables you to easily generate and use your own encryption keys on the AWS Cloud.
- A Hardware Security Module (HSM) provides secure key storage and cryptographic operations within a tamper-resistant hardware device.
- You can use the CloudHSM service to support a variety of use cases and applications, such as database encryption, Digital Rights Management (DRM), Public Key Infrastructure (PKI), authentication and authorization, document signing, and transaction processing.
- To protect and isolate your AWS CloudHSM from other Amazon customers, CloudHSM must be provisioned inside an Amazon VPC.
- CloudHSM works with on-premises HSMs as well.
- CloudHSM publishes multiple CloudWatch metrics for CloudHSM Clusters and for individual HSMs.

AWS Secrets Manager

- AWS Secrets Manager protects access to your applications, services, and IT resources, without the upfront investment and on-going maintenance costs of operating your own infrastructure.

- This service enables you to easily rotate, manage, and retrieve database credentials, API keys, and other secrets throughout their lifecycle.
- Using Secrets Manager, you can secure and manage secrets used to access resources in the AWS Cloud, on third-party services, and on-premises.

AWS Certificate Manager | FREE

- This is a service that lets you easily provision, manage, and deploy public and private Secure Sockets Layer/Transport Layer Security (SSL/TLS) certificates for use with AWS services and your internal connected resources.
- SSL/TLS certificates are used to secure network communications and establish the identity of websites over the Internet as well as resources on private networks.
- AWS Certificate Manager removes the time-consuming manual process of purchasing, uploading, and renewing SSL/TLS certificates for your applications, such as Elastic Load Balancers, Amazon CloudFront distributions, and APIs on API Gateway.
- Public SSL/TLS certificates provisioned through AWS Certificate Manager are free. You pay only for

the AWS resources you create to run your application.

AWS Firewall Manager

- AWS Firewall Manager is a security management service which allows you to centrally configure and manage firewall rules across your accounts and applications in AWS Organization.
- As new applications are created, Firewall Manager makes it easy to bring new applications and resources into compliance by enforcing a common set of security rules.
- Using AWS Firewall manager you can easily roll out AWS WAF rules for your Application Load Balancers, API Gateways, and Amazon CloudFront distributions.
- Using AWS Firewall manager you can easily create AWS Shield Advanced protections for your Application Load Balancers, ELB Classic Load Balancers, Elastic IP Addresses and CloudFront distributions.
- With AWS Firewall Manager, you can enable security groups for your Amazon EC2 and ENI resource types in Amazon VPCs.
- With AWS Firewall Manager, your security team can be notified of threats so they can respond and rapidly mitigate an attack.

- AWS Firewall Manager automatically enforces mandatory security policies that you define across existing and newly created resources.
- Firewall Manager also provides centralized monitoring of DDoS attacks across your organization.
- AWS Firewall Manager is integrated with AWS Organizations so you can enable AWS WAF rules, AWS Shield Advanced protections and security groups for your Amazon VPC across multiple AWS accounts and resources from a single place.

AWS Web Application Firewall (WAF)

- AWS WAF is a web application firewall that helps protect your web applications or APIs against common web exploits that may affect availability, compromise security, or consume excessive resources.
- Gives you control over how traffic reaches your applications by enabling you to create security rules that block common attack patterns, such as SQL injection or cross-site scripting, and rules that filter out specific traffic patterns you define.
- Helps protect web applications from attacks by allowing you to configure rules that allow, block, or monitor (count) web requests based on conditions that you define.

- Once a request for your website meets a condition defined in your rules, AWS WAF instructs the underlying service to either block or allow the request based on the action you define.
- AWS WAF is tightly integrated with Amazon CloudFront and the Application Load Balancer (ALB).
- When you use AWS WAF on Amazon CloudFront, your rules run in all AWS Edge Locations, located around the world close to your end users.
- You can deploy AWS WAF on Amazon CloudFront as part of your CDN solution, the Application Load Balancer that fronts your web servers or origin servers running on EC2, or Amazon API Gateway for your APIs.
- When you use AWS WAF on Application Load Balancer, your rules run in region and can be used to protect internet-facing as well as internal load balancers.
- You can get started quickly using Managed Rules for AWS WAF, a pre-configured set of rules managed by AWS or AWS Marketplace Sellers.
- It works in a pay-as-you-go model.

AWS Shield

- AWS Shield is a managed Distributed Denial of Service (DDoS) protection service that safeguards applications running on AWS.
- A distributed denial of service (DDoS) attack is an attack in which multiple compromised systems attempt to flood a target, such as a network or web application, with traffic.
- A DDoS attack can prevent legitimate users from accessing a service and can cause the system to crash due to the overwhelming traffic volume.
- AWS Shield provides always-on detection and automatic inline mitigations that minimize application downtime and latency, so there is no need to engage AWS Support to benefit from DDoS protection.
- AWS Shield is integrated with Amazon CloudFront, which supports custom origins outside of AWS.
- You can protect your web applications hosted anywhere in the world by deploying Amazon CloudFront in front of your application.
- There are two tiers of AWS Shield:
    - ☐ **AWS Shield Standard:**
        - Defends against most common, frequently occurring network and transport layer DDoS attacks that target your web site or applications.
        - When you use AWS Shield Standard with Amazon CloudFront and Amazon Route

53, you receive comprehensive availability protection against all known infrastructure (Layer 3 and 4) attacks.

- All AWS customers benefit from the automatic protections of AWS Shield Standard, at no additional charge.

☐ **AWS Shield Advanced:**

- Provide higher level of protection for EC2, ELB, Amazon CloudFront, AWS Global Accelerator and Amazon Route 53 resources.
- Provides additional detection and mitigation against large and sophisticated DDoS attacks, near real-time visibility into attacks, and integration with AWS WAF, a web application firewall.
- Gives you 24x7 access to the AWS DDoS Response Team (DRT) and protection against DDoS related spikes.
- You can also enable AWS Shield Advanced directly on an Elastic IP or Elastic Load Balancing (ELB).
- AWS Shield Advanced is a paid service.

AWS Security Hub

- AWS Security Hub gives you a comprehensive view of your high-priority security alerts and security posture across your AWS accounts.
- With Security Hub, you now have a single place that aggregates, organizes, and prioritizes your security alerts, or findings, from multiple AWS services, such as Amazon GuardDuty, Amazon Inspector, Amazon Macie, AWS Identity and Access Management (IAM) Access Analyzer, and AWS Firewall Manager, as well as from AWS Partner solutions.
- AWS Security Hub continuously monitors your environment using automated security checks based on the AWS best practices and industry standards that your organization follows.

Amazon Detective

- Amazon Detective makes it easy to analyze, investigate and visualize to quickly identify the root cause of potential security issues or suspicious activities.
- AWS security services like Amazon GuardDuty, Amazon Macie, and AWS Security Hub as well as partner security products can be used to identify potential security issues or findings.

- Amazon Detective automatically collects log data from your AWS resources and uses machine learning, statistical analysis and graph theory to build a linked set of data that enables you to easily conduct faster and more efficient security investigations.
- Amazon Detective maintains up to a year of aggregated data
- It makes it easily available through a set of visualizations that shows changes in the type and volume of activity over a selected time window, and links those changes to security findings.

AWS Artifact | FREE

- AWS Artifact is your go-to, central resource for compliance-related information that matters to you.
- It provides on-demand access to AWS' security and compliance reports and select online agreements.
- You can use AWS Artifact Reports to download AWS security and compliance documents, such as AWS ISO certifications, Payment Card Industry (PCI), and System and Organization Control (SOC) reports.
- You can use AWS Artifact Agreements to review, accept, and track the status of AWS agreements such as the Business Associate Addendum (BAA).
- All AWS Accounts have access to AWS Artifact.

- An Agreement can have two states:
  - ☐ **Inactive:** An Agreement is in Inactive state if the Agreement has not been accepted by the user or a previously accepted Agreement has been terminated by the user.
  - ☐ **Active:** An Agreement is in Active state if the Agreement has been accepted by the user
- Using AWS Artifact, a user in a master account can automatically accept agreements on behalf of all member accounts in an organization, even as new reports and accounts are added.
- Member account users can view and download agreements.

CHAPTER 15 : AWS Support

AWS Support

- AWS Support provides a mix of tools and technology, people, and programs designed to proactively help you optimize performance, lower costs, and innovate faster.
- All support plans provide 24/7 access to customer service, AWS documentation, whitepapers, and support forums.
- AWS Support Business and Enterprise levels include limited support for common operating systems and common application stack components.
- ***Case Management*** - In the AWS Management Console, you can create three types of customer cases in AWS Support:
  - ☐ **Account and billing support** cases are available to all AWS customers so you can get help with billing and account-related questions.
  - ☐ **Service limit increase** requests are also available to all AWS customers. For

information about the default service quotas, formerly referred to as limits

- ☐ **Technical support** cases connect you to technical support for help with service-related technical issues and, in some cases, third-party applications. If you have a Developer support plan, you can communicate using the web. If you have a Business or Enterprise support plan, you can also communicate by phone or live chat.

- If you have the Basic support plan, you can't create a technical support case.
- There are 4 types of support plans are available in AWS :
  - ☐ **Basic plan** - Basic Support is included for all AWS customers and includes: Customer Service & Communities - 24x7 access to customer service, documentation, whitepapers, and support forums.
  - ☐ **Developer plan** - If you are testing or doing early development on AWS and want the ability to get technical support during business hours as well as general architectural guidance as you build and test.
  - ☐ **Business plan** - If you are running production workloads on AWS and want 24x7 access to technical support from engineers, access to Health API, and contextual architectural guidance for your use-cases.

Enterprise plan - 24x7 technical support ...y engineers, tools and ...omatically manage health of ...t, consultative architectural ...designated Technical Account ... to coordinate access to ...entative programs and AWS ...perts.

... vs Business vs Enterprise

		Developer	Business	Enterprise
		7 Core check	Full set of check	Full set of check
	...rs ...to ...rt ...or ...nd Suppo... ...ND **Service limit increase.** Not included **Technical Support**	Business hours email access to Cloud Support Associates for all services	24x7 phone, email, and chat access to Cloud Support Engineers	24x7 phone, email, and chat access to Cloud Support Engineers
Enhanced Tech Support	Unlimited cases / 1 primary contact	Unlimited cases / 1 primary contact	Unlimited cases / unlimited contacts (IAM supported)	Unlimited cases / unlimited contacts (IAM supported)
Case Severity / Response Times	General guidance: < 24 business hours	General guidance: < 24 business hours System impaired: < 12 business	General guidance: < 24 hours System impaired: < 12 hours	General guidance: < 24 hours System impaired: < 12 hours

		hours	Production system impaired: < 4 hours Production system down: < 1 hour	Production system impaired: < 4 hours Production system down: < 1 hour Business-critical system down: < 15 minutes
Architectural Guidance	N/A	General	Contextual to your use-cases	Consultative review and guidance based on your applications
Programmatic Case Management	N/A	N/A	AWS Support API	AWS Support API
Third-Party Software Support	N/A	N/A	Interoperability & configuration guidance and troubleshooting	Interoperability & configuration guidance and troubleshooting
Proactive Programs	N/A	N/A	Access to Infrastructure Event Management for additional fee.	Infrastructure Event Management Well-Architected Reviews Operations Reviews Technical Account Manager (TAM) coordinates access to programs and other AWS experts as needed.
Technical Account Management	N/A	N/A	N/A	Designated Technical Account Manager (TAM) to proactively monitor your

				environment and assist with optimization.
Training	N/A	N/A	N/A	Designated Technical Account Manager (TAM) to proactively monitor your environment and assist with optimization.
Account Assistance	N/A	N/A	N/A	Concierge Support Team
Pricing	FREE	Greater of $29 / month*** **- or -** 3% of monthly AWS usage See pricing detail and example.	Greater of $100 / month*** **- or -** 10% of monthly AWS usage for the first $0–$10K 7% of monthly AWS usage from $10K–$80K 5% of monthly AWS usage from $80K–$250K 3% of monthly AWS usage over $250K See pricing detail and example.	Greater of $15,000 **- or -** 10% of monthly AWS usage for the first $0–$150K 7% of monthly AWS usage from $150K–$500K 5% of monthly AWS usage from $500K–$1M 3% of monthly AWS usage over $1M See pricing detail and example.

CLOUDAI Coffee Break

"Imagination is everything. It is the preview of life's coming attractions."
- *Albert Einstein*

CHAPTER 16 : AWS Pricing Model

What are the different AWS Pricing Models?

- Pay-as-you-go
- Save when you reserve
- Pay less by using more
- EC2 Pricing model - On-Demand
- EC2 Pricing model - Spot instances
- EC2 Pricing model - Savings Plans
- EC2 Pricing model - Reserved Instances
- EC2 Pricing model - Dedicated Hosts

Pay-as-you-go

- You pay only for the individual services you need, for as long as you use them, and without requiring long-term contracts or complex licensing.
- You only pay for the services you consume, and once you stop using them, there are no additional costs or termination fees.

- You can adapt your business depending on need and not on forecasts, reducing the risk of over positioning or missing capacity.
- By paying for services on an as needed basis, you can redirect your focus to innovation and invention, reducing procurement complexity and enabling your business to be fully elastic.
- You don't have to go for long term contract by praying a large upfront cost
- You are free to add or remove resources anytime

Save when you reserve

- When you buy Reserved Instances, the larger the upfront payment, the greater the discount.
- Certain services like Amazon EC2 and Amazon RDS, you can invest in reserved capacity.
- With Reserved Instances, you can save up to 75% over equivalent on-demand capacity.
- Reserved Instances are available in 3 options:
  - ☐ **All up-front (AURI)** - To maximize your savings, you can pay all up-front and receive the largest discount.
  - ☐ **Partial up-front (PURI)** - Partial up-front RI's offer lower discounts but give you the option to spend less up front.
  - ☐ **No upfront payments (NURI)** - You can choose to spend nothing up front and

receive a smaller discount, but allowing you to free up capital to spend on other projects.

Pay less by using more

- With AWS, you can get volume based discounts and realize important savings as your usage increases.
- services such as S3 and data transfer OUT from EC2, pricing is tiered, meaning the more you use, the less you pay per GB. As a result, as your AWS usage needs increase, you benefit from the economies of scale that allow you to increase adoption and keep costs under control.
- To optimize your savings, choose the right combinations of storage solutions that help you reduce costs while preserving performance, security and durability.

>> Pay even less when AWS grows

- AWS reduces their prices 81 time till date and reduce almost 44% cost

EC2 Pricing model - On-Demand

- On-Demand - With On-Demand instances, you pay for compute capacity by the hour or the second depending on which instances you run
- No longer-term commitments or upfront payments are needed.
- You can increase or decrease your compute capacity depending on the demands of your application and only pay the specified per hourly rates for the instance you use.
- Perfect for the users who prefer the low cost and flexibility of Amazon EC2 without any up-front payment or long-term commitment.
- Can be used for the applications with short-term, spiky, or unpredictable workloads that cannot be interrupted.
- Good for the applications being developed or tested on Amazon EC2 for the first time.

EC2 Pricing model - Spot Instance

- Amazon EC2 Spot instances allow you to request spare Amazon EC2 computing capacity for up to 90% off the On-Demand price.
- Spot Instances is an unused EC2 instance, with which you pay the Spot price that's in effect for the time period your instances are running.

- Spot Instance prices are set by Amazon EC2 and adjust gradually based on long-term trends in supply and demand for Spot Instance capacity.
- Spot Instances are also available to run for a predefined duration – in hourly increments up to six hours in length – at a discount of up to 30-50% compared to On-Demand pricing.
- You can stop and start an Amazon EBS-backed Spot Instance. In addition, the Amazon EC2 Spot service can interrupt an individual Spot Instance if capacity is no longer available,
- The ***Spot Instance advisor*** helps you determine pools with the least chance of interruption and provides the savings you get over on-demand rates.
- This is useful for the applications that have flexible start and end times.
- Useful for the applications that are only feasible at very low compute prices.
- Can be helpful for users with urgent computing needs for large amounts of additional capacity.
- The hourly price for Spot Instances varies based on demand.
- Can only be launched immediately if the Spot Request is active and capacity is available.

EC2 Pricing model - Savings Plans

- Savings Plans is a flexible pricing model that provides savings of up to 72% on your AWS compute usage.
- This pricing model offers lower prices on Amazon EC2 instances usage, regardless of instance family, size, OS, tenancy or AWS Region, and also applies to AWS Fargate and AWS Lambda usage.
- Savings Plans offer significant savings over On Demand, just like EC2 Reserved Instances, in exchange for a commitment to use a specific amount of compute power (measured in $/hour).
- The plan is available for 1 or 3 years period.
- It provides recommendations, performance reporting and budget alerts in the AWS Cost Explorer.

EC2 Pricing model - Reserved Instances

- Amazon EC2 Reserved Instances (RI) provide a significant discount (up to 72%) compared to On-Demand pricing
- Provide a capacity reservation when used in a specific Availability Zone.
- You have the flexibility to change families, OS types, and tenancies while benefiting from RI pricing when you use Convertible RIs.

- RIs can provide a capacity reservation, offering additional confidence in your ability to launch the number of instances you have reserved when you need them.
- If you purchase a large number of RIs in an AWS region, you will automatically receive discounts on your upfront fees and hourly fees for future purchases of RIs in that AWS region.
- RIs are sold by third-party sellers on the Reserved Instance Marketplace.
- RIs are available for 1-year or 3-years contract.
- There are 3 types of RIs:
    - ☐ **Standard RIs** - These provide the most significant discount (up to **72%** off On-Demand) and are best suited for steady-state usage.
    - ☐ **Convertible RIs** - These provide a discount (up to **54%** off On-Demand) and the capability to change the attributes of the RI as long as the exchange results in the creation of Reserved Instances of equal or greater value.

      Like Standard RIs, Convertible RIs are best suited for steady-state usage.
    - ☐ **Scheduled RIs** - These are available to launch within the time windows you reserve.

      This option allows you to match your capacity reservation to a predictable recurring schedule that only requires a fraction of a day, a week, or a month.

EC2 Pricing model - Dedicated Hosts

- A Dedicated Host is a physical EC2 server in AWS dedicated for your use.
- Dedicated Hosts can help you reduce costs by allowing you to use your existing server-bound software licenses, including Windows Server, SQL Server, and SUSE Linux Enterprise Server (subject to your license terms).
- It also helps you meet compliance requirements.
- This can be purchased On-Demand (hourly).
- Can be purchased as a Reservation for up to 70% off the On-Demand price.
- Mostly the customers who don't want to share the physical server with any other customer use this.

EC2 Pricing model - Per Second Billing

- With per-second billing, you pay for only what you use.
- It takes the cost of unused minutes and seconds in an hour off of the bill, so you can focus on improving your applications instead of maximizing usage to the hour.
- If you manage instances running for irregular periods of time, such as dev/testing, data

processing, analytics, batch processing and gaming applications, can benefit.

- EC2 usage are billed on one second increments, with a minimum of 60 seconds.
- Similarly, provisioned storage for EBS volumes will be billed per-second increments, with a 60 second minimum.
- Per-second billing with Hourly rate is available for instances launched in:
  - ☐ On-Demand, Reserved and Spot forms
  - ☐ All regions and Availability Zones
  - ☐ Amazon Linux and Ubuntu
- Per-second is not applicable for any Windows server. It's Hourly billing with Hourly rate.

CLOUDAI Coffee Break

Impressed on your progress.
You are on the right track to be a cloud professional, one of the most demanding profession in current IT and Tech Industry.
And the demand is constantly growing.....

CHAPTER 17 : AWS Cost Management

What are the different AWS Cost Management tools?

- TCO Calculator
- AWS Pricing Calculator
- Economics Resource Center
- AWS Cost Explorer
- AWS Budgets
- AWS Cost & Usage Report
- Reserved Instance (RI) Reporting

TCO Calculator | FREE

- Use this calculator to compare the cost of running your applications in an on-premises or traditional hosting environment to AWS.
- Describe your on-premises or colocation configuration to produce a detailed cost comparison with AWS.

- You can switch between the basic and advanced views to provide additional configuration details.
- The calculators also give you the option to modify assumptions that best meet your business needs.
- Describe your existing or planned on-premises or hosting infrastructure in four steps, or enter detailed configurations.
- Provide an instant graphical summary report which shows you the three year TCO comparison by cost categories.
- Can be download a full report including detailed cost breakdowns, Methodology, Assumptions, and FAQ or store the report in Amazon S3 for sharing with others.
- Customers can use TCO Calculator without having any AWS account.

AWS Pricing Calculator | FREE

- Configure a cost estimate that fits your unique business or personal needs with AWS products and services.
- Create an estimate for the cost of your use cases on AWS.
- You can model your solutions before building them, explore the price points and calculations behind your estimate, and find the available instance types and contract terms that meet your needs.

- Easily calculate your monthly costs with AWS.
- You can create groups of services in different Regions to see how pricing may vary.
- Estimate the cost to migrate your architecture setup to the cloud, or explore what an expansion of your business might look like.
- AWS Pricing Calculator is useful both for people who have never used AWS and for users who want to reorganize or expand their AWS usage.
- You don't need an AWS account or in-depth knowledge of AWS to use AWS Pricing Calculator.
- AWS Pricing Calculator is free for use.

AWS Cost Explorer

- AWS Cost Explorer has an easy-to-use interface that lets you visualize, understand, and manage your AWS costs and usage over time.
- Analyze your data at a high level (for example, total costs and usage across all accounts) or dive deeper into your cost and usage data to identify trends, pinpoint cost drivers, and detect anomalies.
- AWS Cost Explorer includes a default report that helps you visualize the costs and usage associated with your top five cost-accruing AWS services
- It gives you a detailed breakdown on all services in the table view.

- The reports let you adjust the time range to view historical data going back up to twelve months to gain an understanding of your cost trends.
- AWS Cost Explorer helps you visualize, understand, and manage your AWS costs and usage over a daily or monthly granularity.
- The solution also lets you dive deeper using granular filtering and grouping dimensions such as Usage Type and Tags.
- You can also access your data with further granularity by enabling hourly and resource level granularity.
- You can currently save up to 50 custom AWS Cost Explorer reports.
- The Cost Explorer Hourly and Resource level granularity allows you to access hourly granularity for the past 14 days and resource level granularity for EC2 instances.

AWS Cost & Usage Report

- The AWS Cost & Usage Report is your one-stop shop for accessing the most detailed information available about your AWS costs and usage.
- The AWS Cost & Usage Report is updated at least once per day and an updated version of the report is delivered to your S3 bucket each time an update is completed.

- You can configure your Cost & Usage Reports to integrate with Amazon Athena.
- The AWS Cost & Usage Report can also be automatically uploaded into Amazon Redshift and/or Amazon QuickSight.

AWS Billing and Cost Management Dashboard | FREE

- AWS Billing and Cost Management is the service that you use to pay your AWS bill, monitor your usage, and analyze and control your costs.
- AWS automatically charges the credit card that you provided when you signed up for a new account with AWS.
- Charges appear on your monthly credit card bill.
- You can view or update your credit card information, including designating a different credit card for AWS to charge, on the Payment Methods page in the Billing and Cost Management console.
- AWS Billing and Cost Management provides useful tools to help you gather information related to your cost and usage, analyze your cost drivers and usage trends, and take action to budget your spending.

AWS Budgets

- AWS Budgets enable you to plan your service usage, service costs, and instance reservations.
- AWS Budgets information is updated up to three times a day.
- Updates typically occur between 8 to 12 hours after the previous update.
- Budgets track your unblended costs, subscriptions, refunds, and RIs.
- The AWS Budgets Dashboard is your hub for creating, tracking, and inspecting your budgets.
- Budgets provide you with a way to see the following information:
  - ☐ How close your plan is to your budgeted amount or to the free tier limits
  - ☐ Your usage to date, including how much you have used of your Reserved Instances (RIs)
  - ☐ Your current estimated charges from AWS and how much your predicted usage will incur in charges by the end of the month
  - ☐ How much of your budget has been used
- You can create the following types of budgets:
  - ☐ Cost budgets – Plan how much you want to spend on a service.
  - ☐ Usage budgets – Plan how much you want to use one or more services.
  - ☐ RI utilization budgets – This lets you see if your RIs are unused or under-utilized.

- ☐ RI coverage budgets – This lets you see how much of your instance usage is covered by a reservation.
- ☐ Savings Plans utilization budgets – This lets you see if your Savings Plans are unused or under-utilized.
- ☐ Savings Plans coverage budgets – This lets you see how much of your instance usage is covered by Savings Plans.

- If you use consolidated billing in an organization and you own the master account, you can use IAM policies to control access to budgets by member accounts.
- By default, owners of member accounts can create their own budgets but can't create or edit budgets for other users.
- You can create IAM users with permissions that allows them to create, edit, delete, or read budgets in a specific amount.
- A budget is only visible to users with access to the account that created the budget, and has access to budget itself.
- AWS Budgets gives you the ability to set custom budgets that alert you when your costs or usage exceed (or are forecasted to exceed) your budgeted amount.
- You can also use AWS Budgets to set reservation utilization or coverage targets and receive alerts

when your utilization drops below the threshold you define.

- Reservation alerts are supported for Amazon EC2, Amazon RDS, Amazon Redshift, Amazon ElastiCache, and Amazon Elasticsearch reservations.
- You can create up to 20,000 budgets per standalone account or AWS Organizations master account.
- Your first 62 budget days are free of charge each month.

Consolidated Billing | FREE

- You can use the consolidated billing feature in AWS Organizations to consolidate billing and payment for multiple AWS accounts or multiple Amazon Internet Services Pvt. Ltd (AISPL) accounts.
- Every organization in AWS Organizations has a master (payer) account that pays the charges of all the member (linked) accounts.
- One bill – You get one bill for multiple accounts.
- Easy tracking – You can track the charges across multiple accounts and download the combined cost and usage data.
- Combined usage – You can combine the usage across all accounts in the organization to share the volume pricing discounts, Reserved Instance discounts, and Savings Plans.

- No extra fee – Consolidated billing is offered at no additional cost.
- If you have access to the master account, you can see a combined view of the AWS charges that the member accounts incur.
- You also can get a cost report for each member account.
- The pricing benefits of Reserved Instances are shared when the purchasing account is billed under a consolidated billing payer account.
- The instance usage across all member accounts is aggregated in the payer account every month.

CHAPTER 18 : AWS Shared Responsibility Model

What are the different AWS Cost Management tools?

- AWS Shared Responsibility Model
- AWS Shared Control

AWS Shared Responsibility Model

- This shared model can help relieve the customer's operational burden as AWS operates, manages and controls the components from the host operating system and virtualization layer down to the physical security of the facilities in which the service operates.
- The customer assumes responsibility and management of the guest operating system (including updates and security patches), other associated application software as well as the

configuration of the AWS provided security group firewall.

- Security and Compliance is a shared responsibility between AWS and the customer.
- The nature of this shared responsibility also provides the flexibility and customer control that permits the deployment.
- This differentiation of responsibility is commonly referred to as
  - ☐ **Security "of" the Cloud** - AWS is responsible for protecting the infrastructure that runs all of the services offered in the AWS Cloud.

    This infrastructure is composed of the hardware, software, networking, and facilities that run AWS Cloud services.
  - ☐ **Security "in" the Cloud** - Customer responsibility will be determined by the AWS Cloud services that a customer selects.

    This determines the amount of configuration work the customer must perform as part of their security responsibilities. For example, a service such as Amazon Elastic Compute Cloud (Amazon EC2) is categorized as Infrastructure as a Service (IaaS) and, as such, requires the customer to perform all of the necessary security configuration and management tasks.

Customers that deploy an Amazon EC2 instance are responsible for management of the guest operating system (including updates and security patches), any application software or utilities installed by the customer on the instances, and the configuration of the AWS-provided firewall (called a security group) on each instance.

Customers are responsible for managing their data (including encryption options), classifying their assets, and using IAM tools to apply the appropriate permissions.

AWS Shared Control

- This customer/AWS shared responsibility model also extends to IT controls.
- AWS can help relieve customer burden of operating controls by managing those controls associated with the physical infrastructure deployed in the AWS environment that may previously have been managed by the customer.
- As every customer is deployed differently in AWS, customers can take advantage of shifting management of certain IT controls to AWS which results in a (new) distributed control environment.
- Customers can then use the AWS control and compliance documentation available to them to

perform their control evaluation and verification procedures as required. Below are examples of controls that are managed by AWS, AWS Customers and/or both.

- ☐ **Inherited Controls** – Controls which a customer fully inherits from AWS.

  Example : *Physical and Environmental controls*

- ☐ **Shared Controls** - AWS provides the requirements for the infrastructure and the customer must provide their own control implementation within their use of AWS services.

  Controls which apply to both the infrastructure layer and customer layers, but in completely separate contexts or perspectives.

  Example :

  Patch Management – AWS is responsible for patching and fixing flaws within the infrastructure, but customers are responsible for patching their guest OS and applications.

  Configuration Management – AWS maintains the configuration of its infrastructure devices, but a customer is responsible for configuring their own guest operating systems, databases, and applications.

Awareness & Training - AWS trains AWS employees, but a customer must train their own employees.

☐ **Customer Specific** - Controls which are solely the responsibility of the customer based on the application they are deploying within AWS services.

Example - *Service and Communications Protection or Zone Security which may require a customer to route or zone data within specific security environments.*

CLOUDAI Coffee Break

The next Chapter will be a little bit lengthy and conceptual. More than 80% of your preparation is completed. Doing Great

You are almost there…..

CHAPTER 19 : AWS Best Practices and Well-architect-framework

What are the different AWS AWS Best Practices and Well-architect-framework?

- Well-architect-framework
- General Design Principles
- Operational Excellence
- Security
- Reliability
- Performance Efficiency
- Cost Optimization

Well-architect-framework

- The AWS Well-Architected Framework helps you understand the pros and cons of decisions you make while building systems on AWS.
- By using the Framework you will learn architectural best practices for designing and operating reliable,

secure, efficient, and cost-effective systems in the cloud.

- It provides a way for you to consistently measure your architectures against best practices and identify areas for improvement.
- Having well-architected systems greatly increases the likelihood of business success.
- The AWS Well-Architected Framework is based on five pillars :
    - ☐ Operational excellence
    - ☐ Security
    - ☐ Reliability
    - ☐ Performance efficiency
    - ☐ Cost optimization

General Design Principles

- **Stop guessing your capacity needs:**
    - ☐ Eliminate guessing about your infrastructure capacity needs.
    - ☐ You don't have to make a capacity decision before you deploy a system.
    - ☐ Stop worrying about expensive idle resources or dealing with the performance implications of limited capacity.
    - ☐ You can use as much or as little capacity as you need, and scale up and down automatically.
- **Test systems at production scale:**

- ☐ In the cloud, you can create a production-scale test environment on demand, complete your testing, and then decommission the resources.
- ☐ Because you only pay for the test environment when it's running, you can simulate your live environment for a fraction of the cost of testing on premises.

- **Automate to make architectural experimentation easier:**
  - ☐ Automation allows you to create and replicate your systems at low cost and avoid the expense of manual effort.
  - ☐ You can track changes to your automation, audit the impact, and revert to previous parameters when necessary.
- **Allow for evolutionary architectures:**
  - ☐ In the cloud, the capability to automate and test on demand lowers the risk of impact from design changes.
  - ☐ This allows systems to evolve over time so that businesses can take advantage of innovations as a standard practice.
- **Drive architectures using data:**
  - ☐ In the cloud you can collect data on how your architectural choices affect the behavior of your workload.
  - ☐ This lets you make fact-based decisions on how to improve your workload.

- ☐ Your cloud infrastructure is code, so you can use that data to inform your architecture choices and improvements over time.

- **Improve through game days:**
  - ☐ Test how your architecture and processes perform by regularly scheduling game days to simulate events in production.
  - ☐ This will help you understand where improvements can be made and can help develop organizational experience in dealing with events.

Well-Arch-Framework:Operational Excellence

- **Perform operations as code -** You can define your entire workload (applications, infrastructure) as code and update it with code.

  You can implement your operations procedures as code and automate their execution by triggering them in response to events.

  By performing operations as code, you limit human error and enable consistent responses to events.

- **Annotate documentation -** You can automate the creation of annotated documentation after every build (or automatically annotate hand-crafted documentation).

Annotated documentation can be used by people and systems.

Use annotations as an input to your operations code.

- **Make frequent, small, reversible changes** - Design workloads to allow components to be updated regularly.

  Make changes in small increments that can be reversed if they fail (without affecting customers when possible).
- **Refine operations procedures frequently** - As you evolve your workload, evolve your procedures appropriately.

  Set up regular game days to review and validate that all procedures are effective and that teams are familiar with them.
- **Anticipate failure** - Perform "pre-mortem" exercises to identify potential sources of failure so that they can be removed or mitigated.

  Test your failure scenarios and validate your understanding of their impact.

  Test your response procedures to ensure that they are effective, and that teams are familiar with their execution.

  Set up regular game days to test workloads and team responses to simulated events.
- **Learn from all operational failures** - Drive improvement through lessons learned from all operational events and failures.

Share what is learned across teams and through the entire organization.

- **BEST PRACTICES :** There are three best practice areas for operational excellence in the cloud:
    - ☐ **Prepare** - Effective preparation is required to drive operational excellence. Create mechanisms to validate that workloads, or changes, are ready to be moved into production and supported by operations. Operational readiness is validated through checklists to ensure a workload meets defined standards and that

      Example :

        - *AWS Config and AWS Config rules can be used to create standards for workloads and to determine if environments are compliant with those standards before being put into production.*
        - *AWS CloudFormation enables you to have consistent, templated, sandbox development, test, and production environments with increasing levels of operations control.*
    - ☐ **Operate** - Define expected outcomes, determine how success will be measured, and identify the workload and operations metrics that will be used in those calculations to determine if operations are successful. Consider that operational health includes both

the health of the workload and the health and success of the operations acting upon the workload. Routine operations, as well as responses to unplanned events, should be automated.

Example :

- *Amazon CloudWatch allows you to monitor the operational health of a workload.*
- *AWS X-Ray, CloudWatch, CloudTrail, and VPC Flow Logs enabling the identification of workload issues in support of root cause analysis and remediation.*

☐ **Evolve** - Share lessons learned across teams to share the benefits of those lessons. Analyze trends within lessons learned and perform cross-team retrospective analysis of operations metrics to identify opportunities and methods for improvement.

Example :

- *Amazon Elasticsearch Service (Amazon ES) allows you to analyze your log data to gain actionable insights quickly and securely.*

Well-Arch-Framework : Security

- **Implement a strong identity foundation** - Implement the principle of least privilege and enforce separation of duties with appropriate authorization for each interaction with your AWS resources.

  Centralize privilege management and reduce or even eliminate reliance on long-term credentials.
- **Enable traceability** - Monitor, alert, and audit actions and changes to your environment in real time.

  Integrate logs and metrics with systems to automatically respond and take action.
- **Apply security at all layers** - Rather than just focusing on protection of a single outer layer, apply a defense-in-depth approach with other security controls.

  Apply to all layers (e.g., edge network, VPC, subnet, load balancer, every instance, operating system, and application).
- **Automate security best practices** - Automated software-based security mechanisms improve your ability to securely scale more rapidly and cost effectively.

  Create secure architectures, including the implementation of controls that are defined and managed as code in version-controlled templates.
- **Protect data in transit and at rest** - Classify your data into sensitivity levels and use

mechanisms, such as encryption, tokenization, and access control where appropriate.

- **Keep people away from data** - Create mechanisms and tools to reduce or eliminate the need for direct access or manual processing of data.

  This reduces the risk of loss or modification and human error when handling sensitive data.

- **Prepare for security events** - Prepare for an incident by having an incident management process that aligns to your organizational requirements.

  Run incident response simulations and use tools with automation to increase your speed for detection, investigation, and recovery.

- **BEST PRACTICES :**
  - ☐ **Identity and Access Management** - Credentials must not be shared between any user or system. User access should be granted using a least-privilege approach with best practices including password requirements and MFA enforced. Programmatic access including API calls to AWS services should be performed using temporary and limited-privilege credentials such as those issued by the AWS Security Token Service.

    <u>Example :</u>

    - *IAM enables you to securely control access to AWS services and resources.*
    - *MFA adds an additional layer of protection on user access.*

- *AWS Organizations lets you centrally manage and enforce policies for multiple AWS accounts.*

☐ **Detective Controls** - You can use detective controls to identify a potential security threat or incident. They are an essential part of governance frameworks and can be used to support a quality process, a legal or compliance obligation, and for threat identification and response efforts.

Example :

- *AWS CloudTrail records AWS API calls, AWS Config provides a detailed inventory of your AWS resources and configuration.*
- *Amazon GuardDuty is a managed threat detection service that continuously monitors for malicious or unauthorized behavior.*
- *Amazon CloudWatch is a monitoring service for AWS resources which can trigger CloudWatch Events to automate security responses.*

☐ **Infrastructure Protection** -Multiple layers of defense are advisable in any type of environment. In the case of infrastructure protection, many of the concepts and methods are valid across cloud and on-premises models.

Example :

- *Amazon Virtual Private Cloud (Amazon VPC) enables you to launch AWS resources into a virtual network that you've defined.*
- *Amazon CloudFront is a global content delivery network that securely delivers data, videos, applications, and APIs to your viewers which integrates with AWS Shield for DDoS mitigation.*
- *AWS WAF is a web application firewall that is deployed on either Amazon CloudFront or Application Load Balancer to help protect your web applications from common web exploits.*

☐ **Data Protection** - AWS provides multiple means for encrypting data at rest and in transit. AWS builds features into our services that make it easier to encrypt your data.

Example :

- *Services such as ELB, Amazon Elastic Block Store (Amazon EBS), Amazon S3, and Amazon Relational Database Service (Amazon RDS) include encryption capabilities to protect your data in transit and at rest.*
- *Amazon Macie automatically discovers, classifies and protects sensitive data, while AWS Key Management Service (AWS KMS) makes it easy for you to*

create and control keys used for encryption.

☐ **Incident Response** - Even with extremely mature preventive and detective controls, your organization should still put processes in place to respond to and mitigate the potential impact of security incidents.

Example :

- *IAM should be used to grant appropriate authorization to incident response teams and response tools.*
- *AWS CloudFormation can be used to create a trusted environment or clean room for conducting investigations.*
- *Amazon CloudWatch Events allows you to create rules that trigger automated responses including AWS Lambda.*

Well-Arch-Framework : Reliability

- **Test recovery procedures** - You can test how your system fails, and you can validate your recovery procedures. You can use automation to simulate different failures or to recreate scenarios that led to failures before. This exposes failure pathways that you can test and rectify before a real failure scenario, reducing the risk of components failing that have not been tested before.

- **Automatically recover from failure** - This allows for automatic notification and tracking of failures, and for automated recovery processes that work around or repair the failure. With more sophisticated automation, it's possible to anticipate and remediate failures before they occur.
- **Scale horizontally to increase aggregate system availability** - Replace one large resource with multiple small resources to reduce the impact of a single failure on the overall system. Distribute requests across multiple, smaller resources to ensure that they don't share a common point of failure.
- **Stop guessing capacity** - In the cloud, you can monitor demand and system utilization, and automate the addition or removal of resources to maintain the optimal level to satisfy demand without over or under- provisioning.
- **Manage change in automation** - Changes to your infrastructure should be done using automation. The changes that need to be managed are changes to the automation.
- **BEST PRACTICES:**
    - ☐ **Foundations** - Before architecting any system, foundational requirements that influence reliability should be in place. With AWS, most of these foundational requirements are already incorporated or may be addressed as needed.

Example:

- *AWS IAM enables you to securely control access to AWS services and resources.*
- *Amazon VPC lets you provision a private, isolated section of the 23 AWS Well-Architected Framework AWS Cloud where you can launch AWS resources in a virtual network.*
- *AWS Trusted Advisor provides visibility into service limits.*
- *AWS Shield is a managed Distributed Denial of Service (DDoS) protection service that safeguards web applications running on AWS.*

☐ **Change Management -** Being aware of how change affects a system allows you to plan proactively, and monitoring allows you to quickly identify trends that could lead to capacity issues or SLA breaches.

Example:

- *AWS CloudTrail records AWS API calls for your account and delivers log files to you for auditing.*
- *AWS Config provides a detailed inventory of your AWS resources and configuration, and continuously records configuration changes.*

- *Amazon Auto Scaling is a service that will provide an automated demand management for a deployed workload.*
- *Amazon CloudWatch provides the ability to alert on metrics, including custom metrics.*
- *Amazon CloudWatch also has a logging feature that can be used to aggregate log files from your resources.*

☐ **Failure Management** - Being aware of how change affects a system allows you to plan proactively, and monitoring allows you to quickly identify trends that could lead to capacity issues or SLA breaches.

Example:

- *AWS CloudFormation provides templates for the creation of AWS resources and provisions them in an orderly and predictable fashion.*
- *Amazon S3 provides a highly durable service to keep backups.*
- *Amazon Glacier provides highly durable archives.*
- *AWS KMS provides a reliable key management system that integrates with many AWS services.*

Well-Arch-Framework : Performance Efficiency

- **Democratize advanced technologies** - Technologies that are difficult to implement can become easier to consume by pushing that knowledge and complexity into the cloud vendor's domain. Rather than having your IT team learn how to host and run a new technology, they can simply consume it as a service.
- **Go global in minutes** - Easily deploy your system in multiple Regions around the world with just a few clicks. This allows you to provide lower latency and a better experience for your customers at minimal cost.
- **Use serverless architectures** - In the cloud, serverless architectures remove the need for you to run and maintain servers to carry out traditional compute activities.This not only removes the operational burden of managing these servers, but also can lower transactional costs because these managed services operate at cloud scale.

  Example : storage services can act as static websites, removing the need for web servers, and event services can host your code for you.
- **Experiment more often** - With virtual and automatable resources, you can quickly carry out comparative testing using different types of instances, storage, or configurations.

- **Mechanical sympathy** - Use the technology approach that aligns best to what you are trying to achieve.
  Example : consider data access patterns when selecting database or storage approaches.
- **BEST PRACTICES:**
  - ☐ **Selection** - In AWS, resources are virtualized and are available in a number of different types and configurations. This makes it easier to find an approach that closely matches your needs, and you can also find options that are not easily achievable with on-premises infrastructure.
    Example:
    - ***Compute:*** *Auto Scaling is key to ensuring that you have enough instances to meet demand and maintain responsiveness.*
    - ***Storage:*** *Amazon EBS provides a wide range of storage options (such as SSD and provisioned input/output operations per second (PIOPS)) that allow you to optimize for your use case. Amazon S3 provides serverless content delivery, and Amazon S3 transfer acceleration enables fast, easy, and secure transfers of files over long distances.*
    - ***Database:*** *Amazon RDS provides a wide range of database features (such as PIOPS*

and read replicas) that allow you to optimize for your use case. Amazon DynamoDB provides single-digit millisecond latency at any scale.

- ***Network:*** *Amazon Route 53 provides latency-based routing. Amazon VPC endpoints and AWS Direct Connect can reduce network distance or jitter.*

☐ **Review** - When architecting solutions, there is a finite set of options that you can choose from. However, over time new technologies and approaches become available that could improve the performance of your architecture.

Example:

- *The AWS Blog and the What's New section on the AWS website are resources for learning about newly launched features and services.*

☐ **Monitoring** - After you have implemented your architecture you will need to monitor its performance so that you can remediate any issues before your customers are aware. Monitoring metrics should be used to raise alarms when thresholds are breached. The alarm can trigger automated action to work around any badly performing components.

Example:

- *Amazon CloudWatch provides metrics, alarms, and notifications that you can integrate with your existing monitoring solution, and that you can use with AWS Lambda to trigger actions.*

☐ **Trade Offs** - When you architect solutions, think about tradeoffs so you can select an optimal approach. Depending on your situation you could trade consistency, durability, and space versus time or latency to deliver higher performance.

Example:

- *Amazon ElastiCache, Amazon CloudFront, and AWS Snowball are services that allow you to improve performance.*
- *Read replicas in Amazon RDS can allow you to scale read-heavy workloads.*

CLOUDAI Coffee Break

"Imagination is more important than knowledge. Knowledge is limited. Imagination encircles the world."
— Albert Einstein

CHAPTER 20 : AWS Other Services

What are the different AWS Other Services Tools?

- AWS Container
- AWS Mobile
- AWS Media
- AWS Machine Learning
- AWS Internet to Things
- AWS Customer Engagement
- AWS End user computing

AWS Container

- **Amazon Elastic Container Registry (ECR)** - Amazon Elastic Container Registry (ECR) is a fully-managed Docker container registry that makes it easy for developers to store, manage, and deploy Docker container images.

  Integration with AWS Identity and Access Management (IAM) provides resource-level control of each repository.

- **Amazon Elastic Container Service (ECS)** - Amazon Elastic Container Service (Amazon ECS) is a fully managed container orchestration service.

- **Amazon Elastic Kubernetes Service (EKS)** - Amazon Elastic Kubernetes Service (Amazon EKS) is a fully managed Kubernetes service. EKS runs upstream Kubernetes and is certified Kubernetes conformant so you can leverage all benefits of open source tooling from the community.

AWS Mobile

- **AWS Amplify** - AWS Amplify is a development platform for building secure, scalable mobile and web applications.

- **Mobile Hub** - The new AWS Mobile Hub (Beta) simplifies the process of building, testing, and monitoring mobile applications that make use of one or more AWS services.

- **AWS AppSync** - AWS AppSync simplifies application development by letting you create a flexible API to securely access, manipulate, and combine data from one or more data sources.

- **Device Farm** - Improve the quality of your web and mobile applications by testing across desktop browsers and real mobile devices hosted in the AWS Cloud

AWS Media

- **AWS Elastic Transcoder** - Convert digital media stored in Amazon S3 into the audio and video codecs and the containers required by consumer playback devices like mobile, television, web browser etc.

- **AWS Kinesis Video Streams** - Capture, process, and store media streams for playback, analytics, and machine learning.

- **AWS MediaConnect** - High-quality and secured transport service for live video.

- **AWS MediaConvert** - Allows you to easily create video-on-demand (VOD) content for broadcast and multiscreen delivery at scale.
-
- **AWS MediaLive** - The service works by encoding your live video streams in real-time, taking a larger-sized live video source and compressing it into smaller versions for distribution to your viewers.

- **AWS MediaPackage** - Reliably prepares and protects your video for delivery over the Internet.

- **AWS MediaStore** - Store and deliver video assets for live streaming media workflows.

- **AWS MediaTailor** - Insert individually targeted advertising into their video streams without sacrificing broadcast-level quality-of-service.

- **AWS Elemental Appliances & Software** - Encode, package, and deliver video assets on-premises and seamlessly connect with cloud-based video infrastructure.

AWS Machine Learning

- **Amazon SageMaker** - Provides every developer and data scientist with the ability to build, train, and deploy machine learning (ML) models quickly.

- **Amazon CodeGuru** - Machine learning service for automated code reviews and application performance recommendations.

- **Amazon Comprehend** - Natural language processing (NLP) service that uses machine learning to find insights and relationships in text.

- **Amazon Forecast** - Accurate time-series forecasting service, based on the same technology used at Amazon.com

- **Amazon Fraud Detector** - Identify potentially fraudulent online activities such as online payment fraud and the creation of fake accounts.

- **Amazon Kendra** - Easy to use enterprise search service powered by machine learning.

- **Amazon Lex** - Advanced deep learning functionalities of automatic speech recognition (ASR) for converting speech to text, and natural language understanding (NLU) to recognize the intent of the text powered by the same deep learning technologies as Alexa.

- **Amazon Personalize** - Real-time personalization and recommendation, based on the same technology used at Amazon.com.

- **Amazon Polly** - Turns text into lifelike speech, allowing you to create applications that talk.

- **Amazon Rekognition -** Identify objects, people, text, scenes, and activities in images and videos, as well as detect any inappropriate content.

- **Amazon Textract -** Automatically extracts text and data from scanned documents.

- **Amazon Transcribe -** Automatically convert speech to text.

- **Amazon Translate -** Delivers fast, high-quality, and affordable language translation. Allows you to localize content - such as websites and applications - for international users, and to easily translate large volumes of text efficiently.

- **AWS DeepLens -** Deep learning enabled video camera for developers.

- **AWS DeepRacer -** Fastest way to get rolling with reinforcement learning (RL).

- **Amazon Augmented AI -** Amazon A2I makes it easy to build the workflows required for human review of ML predictions.

- **AWS DeepComposer -** Musical keyboard powered by machine learning.

AWS Internet to Things

- **AWS IoT Core** - Easily and securely connect devices to the cloud. Reliably scale to billions of devices and trillions of messages.

- **FreeRTOS** - Real-time operating system for microcontrollers.

- **AWS IoT 1-Click** - Enables simple devices to trigger AWS Lambda functions that can execute an action.

- **AWS IoT Analytics** - Analytics for IoT devices.

- **AWS IoT Device Defender** - Helps you secure your fleet of IoT devices.

- **AWS IoT Device Management** - Register, organize, monitor, and remotely manage connected devices at scale.

- **AWS IoT Events** - Easily detect and respond to events from IoT sensors and applications.
- **AWS IoT Greengrass** - Extends AWS to edge devices so they can act locally on the data they generate, while still using the cloud for management, analytics, and durable storage.

- **AWS IoT SiteWise** - Easy to collect, store, organize and monitor data from industrial equipment at scale.

- **AWS IoT Things Graph** - AWS IoT Things Graph is a service that makes it easy to visually connect different devices and web services to build IoT applications.

AWS Customer Engagement

- **Amazon Connect** - Easy to use omnichannel cloud contact center. Provides a seamless experience across voice and chat for your customers and agents.

- **Amazon Pinpoint** - Amazon Pinpoint enables marketers and developers to deliver customer-centric engagement experiences through multiple channels.

- **Simple Email Service** - Flexible, affordable, and highly-scalable email sending and receiving service for businesses and developers.

AWS End user computing

- **Amazon WorkSpaces** - Desktop-as-a-Service (DaaS) solution. You can use Amazon WorkSpaces to provision either Windows or Linux desktops in just a few minutes and quickly scale to provide thousands of desktops to workers across the globe.

- **Amazon AppStream 2.0** - You centrally manage your desktop applications on AppStream 2.0 and securely deliver them to any computer.

- **Amazon WorkDocs** - Secure content creation, storage, and collaboration service. You can easily create, edit, and share content, and because it's stored centrally on AWS, access it from anywhere on any device.

- **Amazon WorkLink** - A fully managed service that lets you provide your employees with secure, easy access to your internal corporate websites and web apps using their mobile phones.

Well-Arch-Framework : Cost Optimization

- **Adopt a consumption model** - Pay only for the computing resources that you require and increase or decrease usage depending on business requirements, not by using elaborate forecasting.

Example: *Development and test environments are typically only used for eight hours a day during the work week. You can stop these resources when they are not in use for a potential cost savings of 75% (40 hours versus 168 hours).*

- ***Measure overall efficiency*** - Measure the business output of the workload and the costs associated with delivering it. Use this measure to know the gains you make from increasing output and reducing costs.
- ***Stop spending money on data center operations*** - AWS does the heavy lifting of racking, stacking, and powering servers, so you can focus on your customers and organization projects rather than on IT infrastructure.
- **Analyze and attribute expenditure** - The cloud makes it easier to accurately identify the usage and cost of systems, which then allows transparent attribution of IT costs to individual workload owners.

  This helps measure return on investment (ROI) and gives workload owners an opportunity to optimize their resources and reduce costs.
- **Use managed and application level services to reduce cost of ownership** - In the cloud, managed and application level services remove the operational burden of maintaining servers for tasks such as sending email or managing databases.

As managed services operate at cloud scale, they can offer a lower cost per transaction or service.

- **BEST PRACTICES:**
  - ☐ **Expenditure Awareness** - The increased flexibility and agility that the cloud enables encourages innovation and fast-paced development and deployment. . It eliminates the manual processes and time associated with provisioning on-premises infrastructure, including identifying hardware specifications, negotiating price quotations, managing purchase orders, scheduling shipments, and then deploying the resources.

    Example:

    - *AWS Cost Explorer allows you to view and track your usage in detail.*
    - *AWS Budgets notify you if your usage or spend exceeds actual or forecast budgeted amounts.*

  - ☐ **Cost-Effective Resources** - Using the appropriate instances and resources for your workload is key to cost savings. For example, a reporting process might take five hours to run on a smaller server but one hour to run on a larger server that is twice as expensive.

    Example:

- *You can use Cost Explorer for Reserved Instance recommendations, and see patterns in how much you spend on AWS resources over time.*
- *Use Amazon CloudWatch and Trusted Advisor to help right size your resources.*
- *You can use Amazon Aurora on RDS to remove database licensing costs. AWS Direct Connect and Amazon CloudFront can be used to optimize data transfer.*

☐ **Matching supply and demand** - Optimally matching supply to demand delivers the lowest cost for a workload, but there also needs to be sufficient extra supply to allow for provisioning time and individual resource failures.

Example:

- *Auto Scaling allows you to add or remove resources to match demand without overspending*

☐ **Optimizing Over Time** - As AWS releases new services and features, it is a best practice to review your existing architectural decisions to ensure they continue to be the most cost-effective.

Example:

- *The AWS News Blog and the What's New section on the AWS website are resources for learning about newly launched features and services*
- *AWS Trusted Advisor inspects your AWS environment and finds opportunities to save you money by eliminating unused or idle resources or committing to Reserved Instance capacity.*

CLOUDAI Coffee Break

Great Job!!!
You have completed the entire course. You should be super confident about Passing the examination now.
CLOUDAI is super exited to know your success story. Please share your story with us in review comment or Social media platform

Congratulations!!! *for completing the course. At the end of this course you must be fully prepared and confident about your AWS Certified Cloud Practitioner Examination.*

Want to ***evaluate yourself*** *before the final examinations?*

Here are options for you:

1. *Study book of 7 practice test sets with 450+ question*

2. *Exam simulator with 7 practice test sets with 450+ questions* *https://www.udemy.com/course/draft/3200028/?referralCode=B348E042C7DA4CAF1F7F*

Printed in Great Britain
by Amazon

73765839R00135